Wall Quilts

by Marsha McCloskey

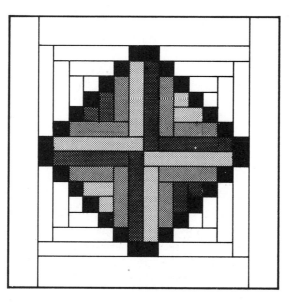

Dover Publications, Inc., New York

in association with

That Patchwork Place ™

Copyright © 1983 by Marsha Reynolds McCloskey.
All rights reserved under Pan American and International Copyright Conventions.

Published in Canada by General Publishing Company, Ltd., 30 Lesmill Road, Don Mills, Toronto, Ontario.
Published in the United Kingdom by Constable and Company, Ltd.

This Dover edition, first published in 1990, is an unabridged republication of *Wall Quilts,* originally published by That Patchwork Place, Bothell, Washington, in 1983.

Manufactured in the United States of America
Dover Publications, Inc., 31 East 2nd Street, Mineola, N.Y. 11501

Library of Congress Cataloging-in-Publication Data

McCloskey, Marsha.
    Wall quilts / by Marsha McCloskey.
        p.   cm.
    Reprint. Originally published: Bothell, WA : That Patchwork Place. c1983.
    Includes bibliographical references.
    ISBN 0-486-26370-3
    1. Quilting. 2. Quilting—Patterns. 3. Wall hangings.
  I. Title.
TT835.M398 1990
746.3—dc20   90-30494
                                                    CIP

Dedicated to my husband, David

Acknowledgments

My thanks to:

   Nancy Dice, whose generous contributions of time and quilting expertise made this book more than it would have been.

   Glendora Hutson, for support and permission to describe her method of finishing a pillow with cording.

   Judy Martin, for encouragement and solid editorial help.

   Pam Boag, Gretchen Engle, and Nancy Martin, for use of quilts and pillows for photography.

   Sharon Yenter, for the use of antique quilts and various photography props from her store.

Nancy Martin and her staff, for making this book possible.

Credits:

Photography	*Carl Murray*
Illustration and Graphics	*Stephanie Benson*

All quilts and pillows made by the author unless otherwise indicated.

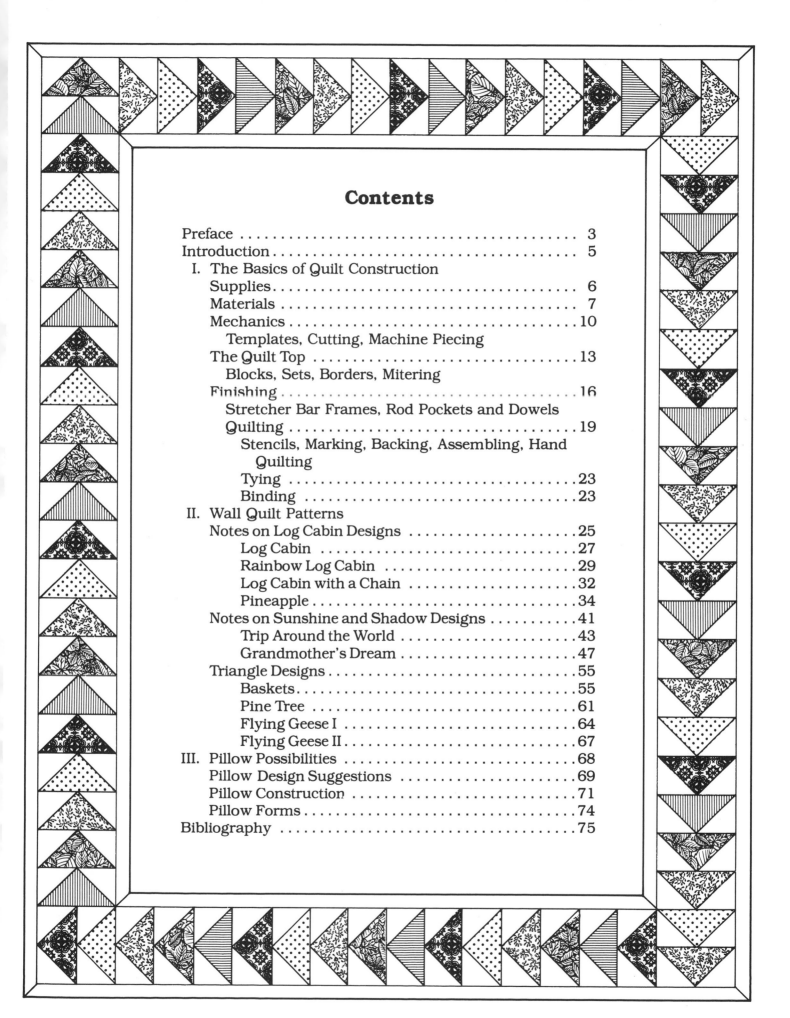

Contents

Preface

There are quilts on the walls in my house. I love to look at them. I change the show frequently. Wall quilts for the seasons and special occasions: red and green for Christmas; warm, patterned and cozy for winter; clean, spare and cool for summer. I am convinced that quilts are good for the soul. A good eyeful of quilt pattern and color in the morning can be as uplifting as flowers in the spring or a sunrise on the mountains.

Traditional quilt designs give us history, culture, home and hearth. Quilts made by family are especially important. A wall quilt you make yourself carries a different meaning in your home and life than any purchased painting or wall piece ever could. Quilts speak to us of our collective and personal history--hardship, perseverance, caring, the good times and the bad, the work ethic, and creating beauty from scraps of fabric and bits of time. I look at my quilts on the wall and know I am part of something important. I am grounded in relationships both cultural and personal. I know who I am.

Woodcut by Nancy Davison

Introduction

WALL QUILTS is a close companion to my first pattern book, **SMALL QUILTS**. The patterns in **SMALL QUILTS** were meant for crib and nap size quilts. But these wall quilts are more decorative than functional. The ten patterns are adaptations of traditional American quilt designs. They are machine pieced and involve only simple, straight seams with hand quilting as an optional finish. Most can be mounted unquilted on wooden stretcher bar frames.

There are three sections in this book. First, "The Basics of Quilt Construction" is the general "how to" section. It includes information on tools and materials, templates and cutting, machine piecing, hand quilting, tying, binding and mounting wall quilts. These methods are simply a description of how I make quilts. Enough guidance is given for a novice quilter to successfully complete the projects. Experienced stitchers may feel more comfortable with other sewing methods. Feel free to personalize any of the designs here. They are offered simply as a starting point. Included with each pattern is a line drawing that can be traced and then colored in different ways. Colors, sizes, sets and borders can all be changed to suit your needs and fancies.

The second section of this book contains the wall quilt patterns, plus special color and piecing tips for each type of pattern presented. Included are Log Cabin designs, Sunshine and Shadow designs, and four patterns that involve lots of triangles. Log Cabin and Sunshine and Shadow patterns are favorites among quilters because they are easy and fun to piece, yet look very complicated. The chain piecing methods described with these designs go very quickly. The piecing techniques take some initial concentration to master, but I think you'll find it worth the effort. The triangle designs, Baskets, Pine Tree and the two Flying Geese, involve the standard machine piecing methods outlined on page 11.

Three of the wall quilts, Baskets, Grandmother's Dream, and Flying Geese II, include quilting designs as well as templates for piecing. These traditional Amish motifs were drafted specially to fit these wall quilts by master quilter Nancy Dice. Her tips on making quilt stencils, marking the quilt top, and quilting with tiny, even stitches are included with the quilting motifs and also in the "how to" section under "Quilting."

Most of the wall quilt designs can be adapted to make patchwork pillows. The third section of this book contains pillow construction details and design ideas.

Happy Quilting!

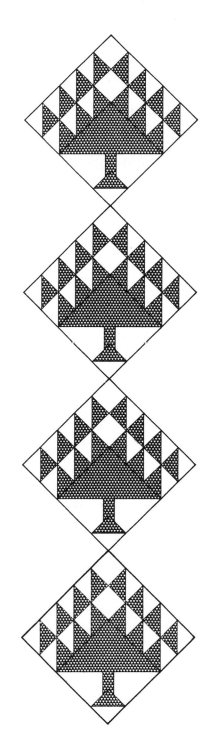

The Basics of Quilt Construction

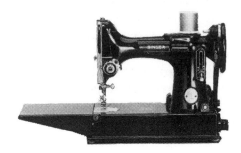

I have been making patchwork quilts and other patchwork items (potholders, pillows, aprons, tea cozies, etc.) for many years. I have sold my work through shops, galleries and craft fairs. When one sews to sell, the work must be done quickly and very well, or no one will buy what you make and you won't get a fair return for your labor and investment. My patchwork production methods have served me well, and I hope to pass some of what I have learned in my years as craftsperson and quiltmaking teacher on to you in this "how to" section.

Even if you are an experienced quiltmaker, read this section to avoid confusion later when I refer to it in pattern instructions.

Supplies

Sewing Machine

It needn't be fancy. All you need is an evenly-locking straight stitch. Whatever kind of sewing machine you have, get to know it and how it runs. If it needs servicing, have it done, or get out the manual and do it yourself. Replace the old needle with a new one. Often, if your machine has a zigzag stitch, it will have a throat plate with an oblong hole for the needle to pass through. You might want to replace this plate with one that has a little round hole for straight stitching. This will help eliminate problems you might have with the edges of fabrics being fed into the hole by the action of the feed dogs.

Scissors

You will need scissors for paper, a good sharp pair for cutting fabric only, and possibly a little pair for snipping threads. If your fabric scissors are dull, have them sharpened. If they are close to "dead", invest in a new pair; it's worth it.

Ruler

A clear plastic ruler, 2" wide and 18" long with a red 1/8" grid on it, is one tool I could not live without. Use it for making templates, measuring and marking borders, and marking quilting lines. If your local quilt shop doesn't carry them, try a stationery store or any place that carries drafting or art supplies. Another useful tool is a 12" plastic 45°/90° right angle.

Marking Pencils

Most marking can be done with a regular #2 lead pencil and a white dressmaker's pencil. Keep them sharp. There is a blue felt tip marking pen available that is water erasable; it works especially well for marking quilting designs. (When you no longer need the lines for guides, dab them with cool water and the blue marks will disappear.) Ask the salespeople at your local fabric or quilt shop about marking pens. There are several different kinds on the market and they will tell you how to use them.

Template Material

1/4" graph paper, tracing paper, lightweight poster board (manila file folders are good) or plastic, and a glue stick.

Seam Ripper

I always keep one handy.

Needles

You'll need an assortment of Sharps for handwork, and quilting needles (Betweens #8, #9 or #10) if you plan to hand quilt. A sharp needle with an eye large enough for sportweight yarn is necessary if you plan to tie.

Pins

Multi-colored glass or plastic headed pins are generally longer, stronger and easier to see and hold than regular dressmakers' pins.

Iron and Ironing Board

A shot of steam is useful.

Staple Gun

If you plan to mount a wall quilt on a wooden stretcher bar frame, you will need a household-weight staple gun with 5/16" sharp pointed staples.

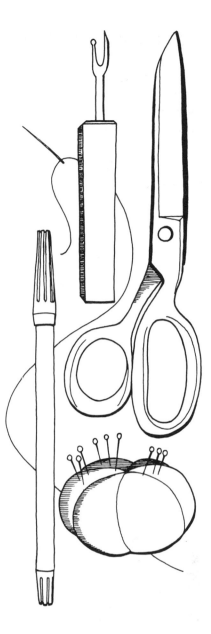

Materials

Fabrics

Before you pick out fabrics, decide which wall quilt to make. Choose a design appropriate in size and shape to your room and wall space. If what you find here isn't just right, perhaps it can be adapted. For instance, make a rectangular wall quilt instead of a square one by adding more rows of unit blocks or taking some away. A square piece can be hung on the diagonal as well as on the horizontal or vertical. A series of three wall quilts could be made to fit a particular space.

I try to keep the size of wall quilts mounted on rigid frames to 36" or smaller. I often take my work to classes and exhibitions, so portability is a consideration. Larger works can be finished as quilts and mounted on the wall with a rod pocket and dowel. (See page 18.)

Vary the visual texture of the prints.

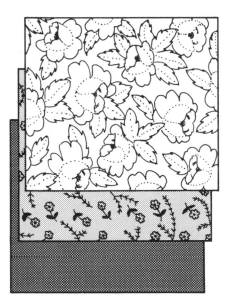

Figure 1. Good fabric selections for three-color quilt designs. Note contrast in color and visual texture.

The fabrics chosen for the designs in this book should be lightweight, closely woven cottons or cotton blends. They should be uniform in weight and have a high cotton content. 100% cottons are best; for patchwork, don't buy fabrics that contain less than 50% cotton. High polyester content makes small patchwork pieces difficult to cut and sew.

Cottons should be preshrunk before use. Even wall quilts collect dirt and if you ever need to wash one, it would be nice to have it come out the same size. Wash light and dark fabrics separately with regular laundry detergent and warm water. A half cup of white vinegar thrown in with the darks is said to help set dyes and prevent them from running or fading later.

Each pattern in this book will give specific information about the fabrics needed to make the design pictured. Log Cabin, Sunshine and Shadow and the Amish-inspired designs all have special color requirements that will be addressed in the pattern section. What follows here are some general guidelines for choosing color and fabrics for quilts.

First, choose a project and a color theme (e.g. earth tones, blue and white, Amish brights, etc.). The colors chosen will depend on where the quilt is to be used and what effect is desired. Choose one fabric that fits the color theme, that you particularly like, and definitely want to use.

This main fabric or "idea print" will give you clues as to what other fabrics will go with it. Think in terms of related colors and contrasts. If your "idea print" is dark, choose something light in a related color to go with it. When two fabrics are side by side, there should be a definite line where one stops and the other begins. This shows contrast.

The contrast should be not only in light and dark, but also in color, the size of the prints and their visual texture. Visual texture is the way a print looks--is it spotty, smooth, plain, dappled, linear, rhythmical or swirly? Are the figures far apart or close together, large or small? Mix large prints with small prints, flowery-all-over designs with little dots or checks. Use solids to add even more variety to the visual texture. Too many similar prints create a dull and uninteresting surface.

Plain, dark solid-looking colors are usually more dominant than lighter, more busy prints and should be placed in the part of the design that you want to stand out. Step back and squint at your fabrics and you should be able to tell which fabrics come forward visually and which recede.

Choose your background fabric carefully. Many quilt patterns have relatively large unpieced areas as background to pieced designs. These areas are generally light in color while the design motif is dark. Good background prints for such designs have subtle all-over texture, fine detail and movement without being spotty or linear. Light solids are too plain for large unbroken areas unless a fair amount of quilting is planned and are better used in small amounts than as main background fabrics.

Figure 2. Using large or widely spaced prints.

Keep in mind that some prints are too large, or have motifs spaced too far apart, to be useful in patchwork with small pieces. The test is this: make a "window" of your fingers the approximate size and shape of the templates you will be using. Move this "window" over the fabric. If the pattern is coherent within the size and shape, then use it. If all you see are blank spaces and parts of flowers, try another fabric with a smaller print. Don't despair though, if you really like the fabric; some widely spaced design motifs can be centered in a piece to achieve a very special effect. Also, large prints can always be used on the backs of quilts.

Another fabric option is to use scraps. Several similar scrap pieces can be substituted for a fabric in a pattern provided they equal roughly the same amount. Log Cabin designs work very well as scrap quilts. It is important when using scraps to maintain good contrast of lights and darks and of visual texture.

Stretcher Bar Frames and Dowels

Wall quilts can be mounted quilted or unquilted on wooden stretcher bar frames which can be purchased at art supply stores, picture frame stores or at some fabric stores. Ready-made stretcher bars come in lengths that increase in two-inch increments (12", 14", 16", etc.). Frame shops will cut them to any size, but it will cost more.

Dowels or flat sticks for hanging quilted and unstretched wall quilts can be found at hardware and art supply stores. A dowel should be thick enough to support the weight of the quilt, but not so thick it makes a noticeable ridge. Curtain rods can also be used.

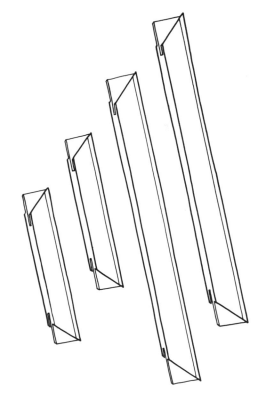

Batting

Batting is the filler in a quilt or comforter. Thick batting is used in comforters that are tied and is not usually appropriate for wall quilts because it is too fluffy to hang well. If you plan to quilt, use thin batting and quilt by hand. Wall quilts can also be tied, but again, use a thin batt.

Thin batts come in 100% polyester, 100% cotton and a cotton-polyester (80%-20%) combination. All-cotton batts require close quilting to prevent shifting and separating in the wash. Most old quilts have cotton batts and are rather flat. Cotton is a good, natural fiber that lasts well and is compatible with cotton and cotton-blend fabrics. 100% polyester batts require much less quilting. If they are glazed or bonded, they are easy to work with, won't pull apart and have more loft than cotton. Some polyester batts, however, have a tendency to "beard." This "fiber migration" (the small white polyester fibers creep to the quilt's surface between the threads in the fabric) happens mostly when polyester blends are used instead of 100% cotton fabrics. The cotton-polyester combination batt is supposed to combine the best features of the two fibers.

The Grandmother's Dream wall quilt pictured on page 39 was quilted by Nancy Dice. She used a single layer of preshrunk cotton flannel for filler instead of batting. The quilt is very flat, and the quilting stitches are highly visible.

Threads

For machine piecing, use white or neutral thread as light in color as your lightest fabric. Use a dark neutral thread for piecing dark solids. 100% cotton thread is easier to work with on some machines.

For hand quilting, use special quilting thread or wax your regular thread. Sportweight yarn or perle cotton is good for tying.

Mechanics

After the quilt design has been chosen, colors thought out, and materials gathered together, the business of cutting and sewing begins. Quiltmaking is a craft that requires close attention, accuracy and patience. It is also centering, relaxing, and practical.

For me there is great joy in watching my quilt designs grow as I sew. The work is fun and will progress smoothly if you are careful and precise about it from the very beginning.

Templates

In patchwork, pattern pieces are called templates. To make your patterns, carefully trace the templates from the book onto graph paper or tracing paper. Trace accurately and transfer to the paper all information printed on the template in the book.

There are two ways to use these templates: use them as paper patterns to cut around, or use them stiffened to trace around before you cut. Paper templates are simply cut out and used. To make stiffened templates, roughly cut out the pattern pieces (outside the cutting line). Glue each one to a thin piece of plastic (x-ray film is good) or lightweight posterboard. Cut out the paper pattern and its stiffening together. Be precise. Make a template for each shape in the design.

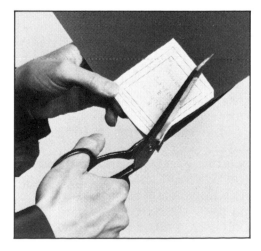

Making a stiffened template

Cutting

Study the design and templates. Determine the number of pieces to cut of each shape and each fabric. Trim the selvage from the fabric before you begin cutting. When one fabric is to be used both for borders and in the unit block designs, cut the borders first and the smaller pieces from what is left over. (See "Borders" on page 14.)

At the ironing board, press and fold the fabric so that one, two or four layers can be cut at one time (except for linear prints like stripes and checks that should be cut one at a time). Fold the fabric so that each piece will be cut on the straight grain.

When using a stiffened template, position it on the fabric so the arrows match the straight grain of the fabric. With a sharp pencil (white for dark fabrics, lead for light ones) trace around the template on the fabric. This is the cutting line. Cut just inside this line to most accurately duplicate the template.

For a paper template, line it up with the straight grain of fabric. Hold it in place on the fabric and cut around it. Be precise. Compare cut pieces with the template to be sure they are true.

In machine piecing there are no drawn lines to guide your sewing. The seam line is 1/4" from the cut edge of the fabric so this outside edge must be precisely cut to insure accurate sewing.

Always make one sample block of a design before embarking on a large project. After cutting the necessary number of pieces of each color and shape for one unit block, arrange the pieces on a flat surface in the desired design. This will help you determine which pieces to sew together first and evaluate your fabric choices and arrangement.

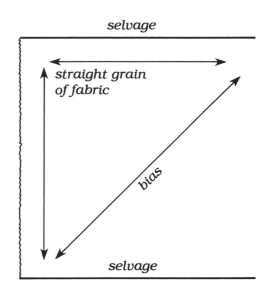

Figure 3. Bias

Using a paper template

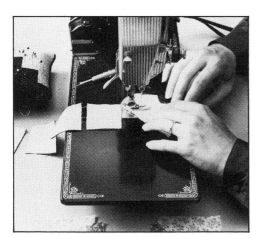

Chain piecing

Machine Piecing

Sew exactly 1/4" seams. To determine the 1/4" seam allowance on your machine, place a template under the presser foot and gently lower the needle onto the seam line. The distance from the needle to the edge of the template is 1/4". Lay a piece of masking tape at the edge of the template to act as the 1/4" mark; use the edge as a guide. Stitch length should be set at 10-12 stitches per inch. For most of the sewing in this book, sew from cut edge to cut edge (exceptions will be noted). Backtack if you wish, although it is not really necessary as each seam will be crossed and held by another.

Use chain piecing whenever possible to save time and thread. To chain piece, sew one seam, but do not lift the presser foot. Do not take the piece out of the sewing machine, and do not cut the thread. Instead, set up the next seam to be sewn and stitch it as you did the first. There will be a little twist of thread between the two pieces. Sew all the seams you can at one time in this way, then remove the "chain." Clip the threads. I use special chain piecing techniques for Log Cabin and Sunshine and Shadow designs. Further instructions for piecing those designs are found with the patterns on pages 25 and 44.

Press the seam allowances to one side, toward the darker fabric when possible. Avoid too much ironing as you sew because it tends to stretch biases and distort fabric shapes.

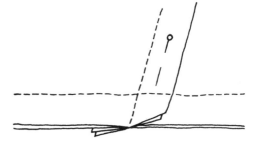

Figure 4. Opposing Seams

Figure 5. Positioning Pin

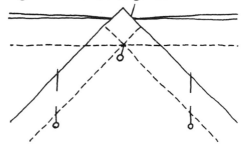

Figure 6. The "X"

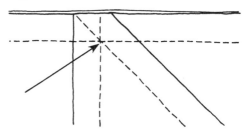

To piece a unit block, sew the smallest pieces together first to form units. Join smaller units to form larger ones until the block is complete. Pay close attention to the design drawing and sewing instructions given with the patterns.

Short seams need not be pinned unless there is matching involved, or the seam is longer than 4". Keep pins away from the seam line. Sewing over pins tends to burr the needle and makes it hard to be accurate in tight places.

Ideally, if pieces are cut and sewn precisely, patchwork designs will come out flat and smooth with crisply matched corners and points. In practice, it doesn't always happen that way. Here are four matching techniques that can be helpful in many different piecing situations.

1. Opposing Seams: When stitching one seamed unit to another, press seam allowances on the seams that need to match, in opposite directions. (See Figure 4.) The two "opposing" seams will hold each other in place and evenly distribute the bulk. Plan your pressing to take advantage of opposing seams.

2. Positioning Pin: A pin, carefully pushed straight through two points that need to match, and pulled tight, will establish the proper point of matching. Pin the seam normally and remove the positioning pin before stitching. (See Figure 5.)

3. The "X": When triangles are pieced, stitches will form an "X" at the next seam line. Stitch through the center of the "X" to make sure the points on the sewn triangles will not be chopped off. (See Figure 6.)

4. Easing: When two pieces to be sewn together are supposed to match but instead are of slightly different lengths, pin the points of matching, and stitch with the shorter piece on top. The feed dogs will ease the fullness of the bottom piece.

You can do beautiful and accurate piecing on the sewing machine. Try to correct mistakes when they happen (keep a seam ripper handy), but don't spend too much time ripping out and resewing. Some sewing inaccuracies are correctable, some are not. Sometimes the best thing is to move on and make the next block better. The quality of your piecing will improve as you go along.

The Quilt Top

Blocks

Most traditional American quilt designs are made up of repeated small designs called unit blocks. There are thousands of unit block designs and they all have names, some historically colorful, some obscure. The wall quilts in this book are named for their unit blocks; thus, we have Log Cabin, Pineapple, and Pine Tree. The Sunshine and Shadow quilts are called one-patch designs. They have design units, but not conventional blocks.

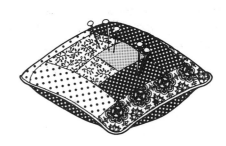

Sets

When unit blocks are sewn together to make a quilt top, it is called the "set". Blocks can be set together side by side, or separated by unpieced blocks or lattice strips which are called "set pieces." The set can be straight on or diagonal. Unit blocks are set together in rows with their set pieces. The rows are then sewn together in sequence to complete the pieced section of the quilt top.

Figure 7.
Assembly sequence for Baskets wall quilt. Diagonal set.

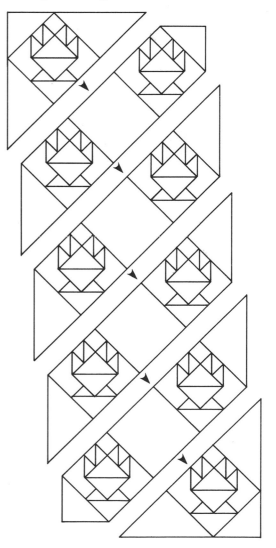

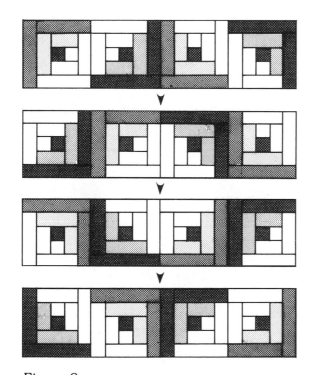

Figure 8.
Assembly sequence of Log Cabin wall quilt. Blocks set adjacently, straight on.

Borders

Borders function as a frame to a quilt design. Each of the wall quilt designs in this book have directions for one type of border treatment. You can make a different border than the one shown. Simply find the border treatment that you prefer on a different quilt and use those border directions on the quilt you're making (adjusting measurements if necessary). You will find simple borders with straight-sewn corners (see Figure 10) and single striped or multiple plain borders with mitered corners (see Figure 9).

For plain borders with straight-sewn corners, first sew borders to the long side of the quilt, then to the width. Striped fabrics make lovely quilt borders, but the corners must be mitered to make the design turn the corner gracefully. Mitered corners are not difficult to do and are worth the effort in some design situations. Miter corners when using stripes or multiple plain borders.

Most border strips for these projects can be cut from the 45" width of yardage, then sewn together to get the proper length if necessary. Seams should be pressed open and placed in the center of the side of the quilt for minimum visibility. Yardages for most borders in this book will be given for border strips cut and pieced in this manner. If you are using a stripe for a border, it is best not to piece it. You will need to buy fabric the length of the longest outside border plus about 4" to allow for shrinkage. It is often wise when cutting border strips to leave them 3 or 4 inches longer than the length given in the pattern. When the actual dimensions of the quilt top are known, the border strips can be trimmed to fit.

Figure 9. Baskets wall quilt with multiple plain borders and mitered corners.

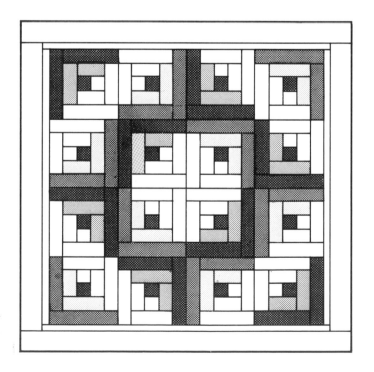

Figure 10.
Log Cabin wall quilt with plain borders and straight sewn corners.

14

Figure 11.

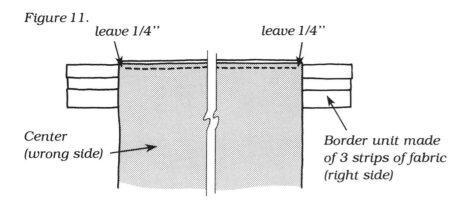

leave 1/4"   leave 1/4"

Center
(wrong side)

Border unit made
of 3 strips of fabric
(right side)

Figure 12.

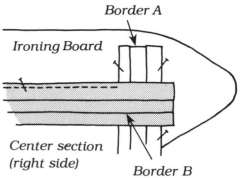

Border A

Ironing Board

Center section
(right side)

Border B

Mitering

To miter corners follow these instructions:

1. Prepare borders. Determine the finished outside dimensions of your quilt. Cut borders this length plus 1/2" for seam allowance. When using striped fabric for borders, make sure the design on all four borders is cut the same way. Multiple borders should be sewn together and the resulting "striped" units treated as a single border for mitering. (See Figure 11.)

2. To attach borders to the pieced section of the quilt, center each border on a side so the ends extend equally on either side of the center section. Using 1/4" seam allowance, sew border to the center leaving 1/4" unsewn at the beginning and end of stitching line. Press seam allowance toward borders. (See Figure 11.)

3. Arrange the first corner to be mitered on the ironing board as pictured. (See Figure 12.) Press it flat and straight. To prevent it from slipping, pin the quilt to the ironing board. Following Figure 13, turn Border "B" right side up, folding the corner to be mitered under at a 45° angle. Match the raw edges underneath with those of Border "A". Fuss with it until it looks good. The stripes and border designs should meet. Check the squareness of the corner with a right angle. Press the fold. This will be the sewing line. Pin the borders together to prevent shifting and unpin piece from board. Turn wrong side out and pin along fold line readjusting if necessary to match designs. (See Figure 14.)

4. Machine baste from inside to outside corner on the fold line, leaving 1/4" at the beginning unsewn. Check for accuracy. If it's right, sew again with regular stitch. Backtack at the beginning and end of the stitch line. (After you've mitered several times, the basting step ceases to be necessary.) Trim excess fabric to 1/4" along mitered seam. Press open. Press other seams to outside. (See Figure 15.)

Figure 13.

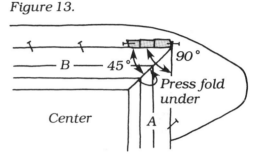

B ——— 45°   90°

Press fold
under

Center   A

Figure 14.

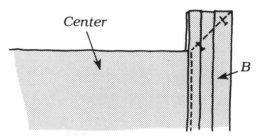

Center

B

Figure 15.

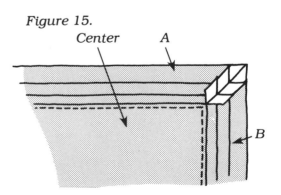

Center   A

B

Finishing

Wall quilts can be finished and mounted in several different ways:
- -Unquilted on a stretcher bar frame;
- -Quilted, and then mounted on a stretcher bar frame;
- -Quilted and finished with bias binding like a regular quilt, then hung with a rod pocket and dowel;
- -Tied (to the back), finished with bias binding and hung as above.

The method you choose for finishing your pieced design will depend on how the piece is to be used, how much time you want to put into the project, and how flat the piecing turns out to be.

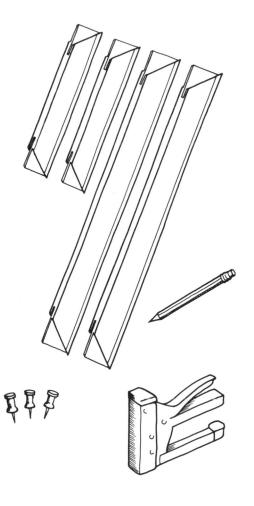

Stretcher Bar Frames

Many patchwork blocks and small quilts can be mounted as described here. If a piece is to be mounted unquilted, the piecing must be very flat. Log Cabin and Sunshine and Shadow designs are good because all the pieces are cut with the straight grain of fabric and there are no biases to pull and pucker when the piece is stretched. When making wall quilts, it might be wise to put off cutting borders and purchasing frames or dowels until the actual piecing is completed and an assessment can be made of the "stretchability" of the patchwork. If your piecing is a little wavy or if there are many triangles in the design, it can still be mounted on a stretcher bar frame, but it will probably need to be hand quilted first. The quilting, not the seams, then takes the stress of "stretching."

To mount your wall quilt on a stretcher bar frame, you will need unbleached muslin lining material, a marking pencil, push pins, the wooden frame and a staple gun. Proceed as outlined below.

1. Make the pieced design and add borders. (See "Borders" on page 14.) These should extend 2 1/2" to 3" beyond the frame on all sides to allow enough fabric to be wrapped around the outside edge of the frame and be stapled down. Press the quilt top. Cut a piece of unbleached muslin lining the same size as the top. If you are going to quilt your hanging and stretch it too, cut a piece of thin batting that extends only 1" beyond the frame edge, not to the edge of the borders. Quilt the piece before it is stretched. (See "Quilting" on page 19.) For an unquilted piece, press and pin baste the muslin lining to the wrong side of the wall quilt top.

2. Assemble the wooden stretcher bar frame. Squeeze the notched corners together to form a square or rectangle. Check the corners with a right angle. Put a staple across each joint. (Figure 16.)

16

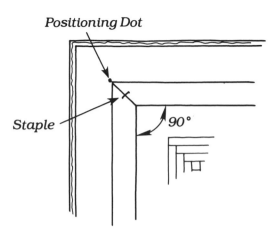

Positioning Dot

Staple

90°

Figure 16.

3. Place the lined wall quilt face up on a large table or on the floor. Place the wooden frame on top and center the design through the "window" formed by the frame. When it is properly positioned, make a dot on the fabric with a marking pencil at each outside corner of the frame.

4. After marking, place the wall quilt face up on top of the frame. Match the positioning dots with the corners of the frame. To hold the hanging in place for stapling, put push pins through the fabric along the outside edge of the frame. Pull the fabric gently across the frame so it is flat and there is no slack. Don't try to stretch it tightly, as too much pulling will distort the seam lines. (Figure 17.)

5. With the wall quilt pinned to the frame, turn it face down. While folding the raw edges under, staple the border fabric to the frame on the side that will face the wall. Start with one staple in the middle of each side. Working from the center out, place staples two to three inches apart on the first side. Stop two inches from each corner. Next, staple the opposite side, then the other two. To finish, trim away a little of the excess fabric at the corners, neatly fold what's left, and staple in place. (Figure 18.)

Figure 17.

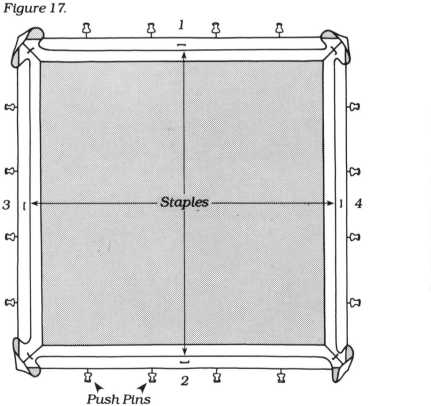

1

3

Staples

4

2

Push Pins

Figure 18.

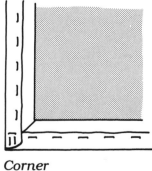

Corner

17

Figure 19.

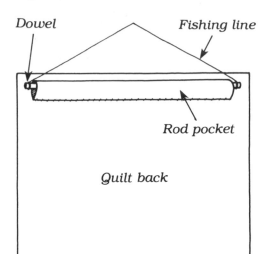

Dowel   Fishing line

Rod pocket

Quilt back

Figure 20. Side view of rod pocket

Rod Pockets and Dowels

For larger quilted pieces, I often use the rod-pocket-and-dowel method for hanging. A rod pocket or "quilt sleeve" is an open-ended fabric tube that is hand stitched to the upper back edge of a quilt. A dowel, flat stick, or curtain rod can be slipped through the fabric tube to evenly support the weight of the quilt when it is hung. Depending on the size of the piece and the condition of the wall, the dowel, stick or rod is then secured to the wall with brackets, nails, hooks and fishing line, or whatever other support seems appropriate. We live in an older home that has wooden molding on the wall about a foot from the ceiling. I hang my quilts from molding hooks with fishing line tied to the ends of dowels that have been inserted in the rod pockets. This system makes it easy to change the "quilt show" as I please. Quilt exhibitions often require quilts for display to have rod pockets; first, for ease of hanging and second, to protect the quilts from the stress and possible tearing that pins, staples or tacks can cause.

To make a rod pocket for your quilt, you will need muslin or fabric to match the quilt backing. Cut a piece 8 1/2" wide and as long as the top edge of the quilt. Fold the piece lengthwise wrong side out. Sew the long raw edges together with a 1/2" seam. Leave the two ends open. Turn the resulting fabric tube right side out and press. Hem the ends so the rod pocket extends only to one inch from each side of the quilt. (Figure 19.)

Figure 20 shows a side view of a rod pocket sewn to the top edge of a quilt. Notice that it is not flat. The side of the rod pocket that is away from the quilt has more fullness to accommodate the bulk of the dowel and the quilt hangs flat. To sew your rod pocket to the quilt in this manner, press the pocket with the seam at the bottom and a crease at the top. Press in another crease 3/4" to 1" from the first one. Position the rod pocket on the quilt with the first crease along the top edge. Pin it in place so you can hand stitch the pocket to the back of the quilt along the second crease and the bottom seam. See figure 20. Sew only through the quilt backing. No stitches should show on the quilt front.

If a quilt is very wide and you are afraid its weight will cause the dowel to bow or break, make the rod pocket in two sections. Extra support can then be added in the middle of the quilt.

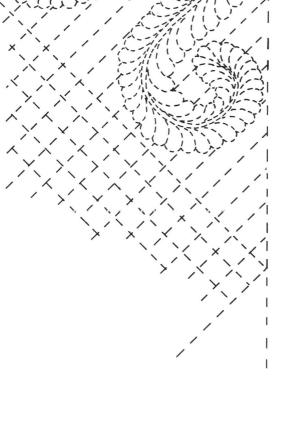

Quilting

A wall quilt is a good place to showcase intricate hand quilting. Quilts mounted on stretcher bar frames and pillow tops provide excellent opportunities to practice quilting skills. Knots can be left on the backs of these one-sided projects, so starting and stopping is much easier than on a quilt where the back must look nice, too. Wall quilts are usually small, requiring a limited amount of quilting time. And, if you hang your quilt on the wall, no one will sit on all that fancy stitching!

After I had pieced the two Amish-inspired wall quilts, Baskets and Grandmother's Dream (pictured on page 39 and the cover), I asked Nancy Dice, friend and experienced quilter, to design appropriate Amish-looking quilting motifs. She had just taken a workshop from Sandi Fox (a well-known quilting expert) on Amish quilting, and was eager to try some of the techniques she had learned. Nancy drafted a Feather Wreath and Plume, Chevrons and Pumpkin Seeds, Ocean Waves and a quilted basket pattern specially to fit these wall quilts. Her useful tips on making stencils, marking quilting lines, and making tiny, even quilting stitches will help you proceed with confidence. The designs appear intricate and closely spaced, and are in keeping with Amish tradition. The techniques involved are simple and straight forward; quilting in the Amish style just takes more time.

Notice that the Feather Wreath designed by Nancy for the Grandmother's Dream wall quilt is also sized to fit the Flying Geese II quilt on page 67.

In most cases, before you hand quilt, the quilt top must be marked with lines to guide your stitching. Where you place the quilting lines will depend on the quilt top design, the type of batt used, and how much quilting you want to do. Feel free to simplify the quilting designs provided here or use other finishing techniques as outlined on page 16. If you don't enjoy quilting Feather Wreaths and Plumes, mark the quilt top with an all-over, straight-line pattern such as a grid of squares or parallel diagonal lines. Or, you can outline quilt the design either "in the ditch" (close to, but not on the seam lines) or 1/4" away on each side of every seam line, for which no marking is required. Try to avoid quilting too close to the seam lines where the bulk of seam allowances might slow you down or make the stitches uneven. Keep in mind also that the purpose of quilting, beside its esthetic value, is to securely hold the three layers of the quilt together. Don't leave large areas unquilted.

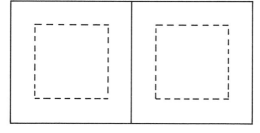

Figure 21. Outline quilting, 1/4" away from seam lines.

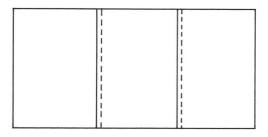

Figure 22. "In the ditch"

Quilting Stencils

There are many pretty, traditional quilting motifs that fit nicely in plain areas like unpieced blocks and borders. You can buy quilt stencils or you can make your own. The instructions below tell how to make stencils to transfer the quilting motifs in this book to your quilt top.

To make quilting stencils, you will need a sharp pencil, tracing paper, carbon paper, lightweight cardboard (manila file folders are good), sharp-pointed scissors, curved fingernail scissors and perhaps a razor blade or other fine sharp cutting tool.

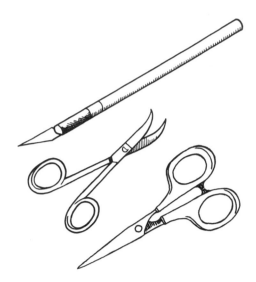

1. With a sharp pencil, trace the quilting motif from the book onto tracing paper. Include positioning lines as well. Notice that the shaded areas are meant to be cut out. The dotted lines will be drawn freehand on the fabric or with a ruler after part of the quilting lines and the basic shapes have been established with the stencil.

2. To transfer the design from the tracing paper to the cardboard, place carbon paper between the two and carefully trace over the lines.

3. With your cutting tools, cut out the areas of the design marked "cut out." Cut just outside the lines to be sure the inside shape is large enough to allow for the width of the pencil line.

Marking the Quilt Top

Thoroughly press the quilt top and mark it before it is assembled with the batt and backing. You will need marking pencils, a long ruler or yardstick, stencils or templates for quilting motifs, and a smooth, clean, hard surface to work on. Use a sharp marking pencil and lightly mark the quilting lines on the fabric. No matter what kind of marking tool is used, light lines will be easier to remove than heavy ones. If you are using the quilting patterns provided here, position the stencils on the quilt top according to the illustrations given, and trace the cut-out shapes onto the fabric. Remember that not all the quilting lines will be drawn using the stencil. The dotted lines on the stencil patterns in the book need to be drawn freehand (for curves) on the fabric or with a ruler (for straight lines). Nancy Dice has provided specific instructions for marking her quilting designs. These helpful hints can be found on pages 50 and 58.

Figure 23. Marking quilting lines with a stencil.

Preparing the Backing

A single length of 45"-wide fabric can often be used for the backing for small quilts. To be safe, plan only on a usable width of 42" after shrinkage and cutting off selvages. For larger quilts, two lengths of fabric will have to be sewn together to get one large enough to serve.

Cut the backing an inch larger all the way around than the quilt top. Press thoroughly with seams open. Lay the backing face down on a large, clean flat surface. With masking tape, tape the backing down (without stretching) to keep it smooth and flat while you are working with the other layers.

Assembling the Layers

If the wall quilt is to be finished with a binding, cut the batt the same size as the backing and lay it on top. Smooth it out as well as you can. Batting for wall quilts to be mounted on wooden stretcher bar frames should extend 1" beyond the edge of the wooden frame, not all the way to the edge of the fabric borders.

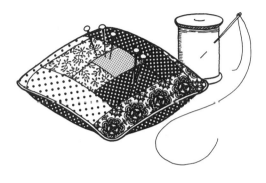

Center the freshly ironed and marked quilt top face up on top of the batting. Starting in the middle, pin baste the three layers together while gently smoothing out fullness to the sides and corners. After pinning, baste the layers together with needle and light-colored thread. Start in the middle and make radiating lines of stitches.

After basting, remove the pins. Now you are ready to quilt. (Figure 24.)

Figure 24. Setting up to quilt

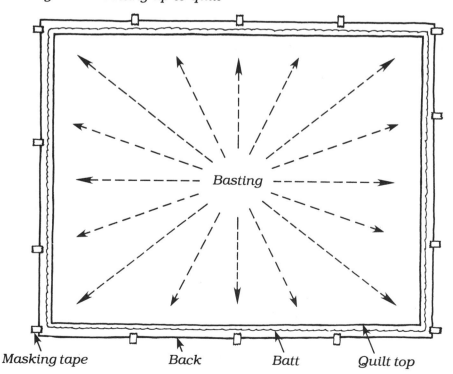

Masking tape   Back   Batt   Quilt top

Hand Quilting

To quilt by hand, you will need quilting thread, quilting needles, small scissors, a thimble and perhaps a balloon or large rubber band to help grasp the needle if it gets stuck. Quilt on a frame, a large hoop, or just on your lap or a table. Use a single strand of quilting thread no longer than 18". Make a small single knot in the end of the thread. The quilting stitch is a small running stitch that goes through all three layers of the quilt. Take two, three or even four stitches at a time if you can keep them even. When crossing seams, you might find it necessary to "hunt and peck" one stitch at a time.

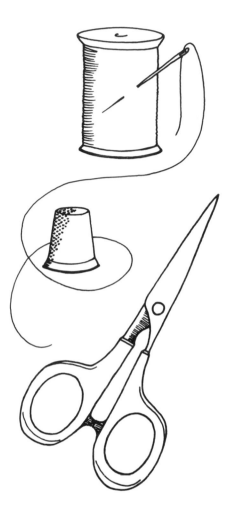

To begin, insert the needle in the top layer about 3/4" from the point you want to start stitching. Pull the needle out at the starting point and gently tug at the knot until it pops through the fabric and is buried in the batting. Make a backstitch and begin quilting. Stitches should be tiny (8 to 10 per inch is good), even and straight. At first, concentrate on even and straight; tiny will come with practice. Several factors will influence how well you do: the size of the needle (a #9 is good, #10 is better), the thickness of the quilt (weight of the fabrics, batting, and whether you are going over seams), and the tension of the piece. If the tension is too tight, the stitches tend to get too large and far apart; too loose, and the lines get crooked. Make some test stitches until you find the proper tension. If you quilt on your lap, you can keep the tension right by holding the piece down between your sewing hand and knee or table while you stitch.

When you come almost to the end of the thread, make a single knot fairly close to the fabric. Make a backstitch to bury the knot in the batting. Run the thread off through the batting and out the quilt top. Snip it off. (Figure 25.) Starting and stopping many times in a quilting design can be tedious, time consuming and difficult to hide. The first and last backstitches look different than the running stitches between. To make them less noticeable, start and stop where quilting lines cross each other or at seam joints. Even so, some designs (e.g. Feather Wreaths and Plumes) require many starts and stops. And you should not run the needle inside the batting for more than its own length to get to a new starting point. After you have worked on a quilting design for awhile, you will discover a sequence for putting in the stitches that requires fewer starts and stops. For the Feather Wreath and Plume designs (patterns begin on page 50), Nancy suggests quilting the double stem in the center first; then the inner and outer scallop lines; and the leaf curves last.

Figure 25. Hand Quilting Stitch

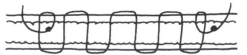

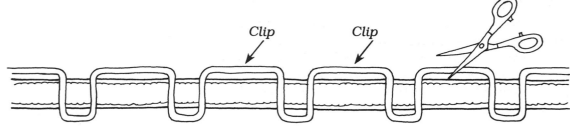

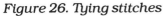

Clip   Clip

Figure 26. Tying stitches

Tying

Wall quilts that are not mounted on stretcher bar frames can be tied instead of quilted. Use a thin batt and tie to the back so the strings won't show. Put the quilt "sandwich" together as for quilting, but instead of basting, insert pins at each point you want a tie. To tie, use a large, sharp needle and perle cotton or sportweight yarn in a color that won't show too much on the top. Cut a long (2-3 foot) piece and make a stitch through the three quilt layers where the first tie is to be. Don't cut the thread yet, but skip over and make a stitch at the next tie location and so on until you run out of thread in your needle. (Figure 26.) Snip the thread between the stitches and tie square knots. (Figure 27.) After tying, trim excess batting and backing, and bind the quilt edges as described below.

Figure 27. Square knot

Binding

The raw edges of wall quilts not mounted on stretcher bar frames need to be bound. After quilting or tying, trim excess batting and backing to the edge of the quilt front. Finish the raw edges with bias binding. Bias binding can be purchased by the package or yard, or you can make it from fabric.

To make bias binding from yardage, press a single layer of fabric. Use a 12" right angle to establish the bias (45° angle) of the fabric by aligning one of the angle's short sides with the selvage. Draw a line on the fabric along the 45° angle. Using this first marked line as a guide, draw several more parallel lines each 2" apart. You'll find the 2"-wide plastic ruler very handy for this procedure. Cut the strips and seam them together where necessary to get a bias strip long enough for each side of the quilt (the length of the side plus 2").

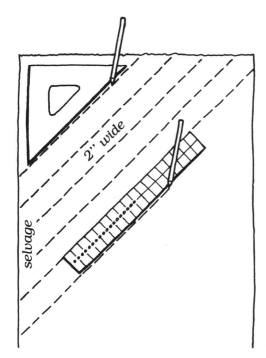

Figure 28. Marking bias strips

Figure 29. Joining bias strips

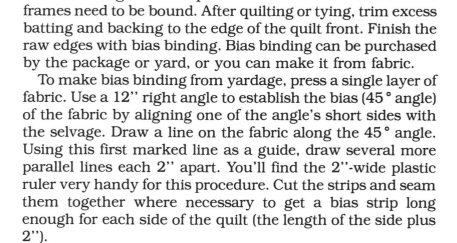

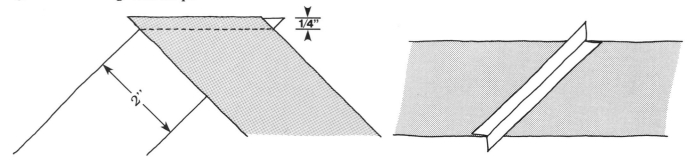

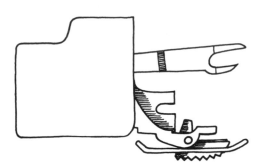

If you have a special sewing machine attachment for sewing through several layers, use it to sew the binding to the quilt edge. Check with your sewing machine dealer to see if an "even-feed" or "walking" foot is available for your machine. It is well worth the trouble. A regular presser foot pushes the top layer of fabric along faster than the ones beneath, and tends to pucker and pleat the piece as you sew. An "even-feed" or "walking" foot feeds all three layers smoothly and evenly.

Using the "even-feed" foot and a 1/2" seam allowance, sew the binding strips to the front of the quilt. Be careful not to stretch the bias or the quilt edge as you sew. If your machine doesn't have an "even-feed" foot, sometimes it is best to put the binding on entirely by hand. Overlap the corners. (See Figure 30.) Fold under the raw edge of the binding on the back side of the quilt. Pin it in place. Enclose the raw edges at the corners. (See Figure 31.) Using thread to match the binding, hand sew the binding in place with a hemming stitch. (See Figure 32.)

Figure 30. Overlapping bias binding at quilt corners.

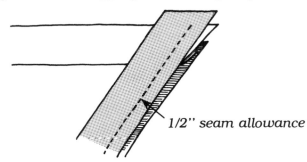

1/2" seam allowance

Figure 31. Quilt corners

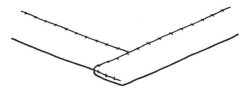

Figure 32. Hemming stitch

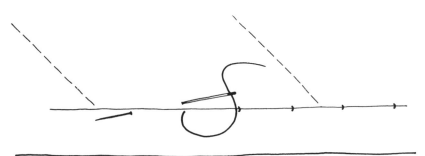

Wall Quilt Patterns

Notes on Log Cabin Designs

The Log Cabin, a long-time quilter's favorite, is especially well suited for mounting unquilted on a wooden stretcher bar frame. Technically, it has no biases and the piecing usually comes out flat and smooth. Graphically, Log Cabin designs look complicated without being quilted. The Log Cabins in this book, with the exception of the Rainbow Log Cabin, depend on the placement of groups of light and dark fabrics to achieve an all-over quilt design. Each unit block has a group of light prints, a group of dark prints, and one accent color that usually is a medium or dark solid. The center square is the solid fabric, and traditionally is the same for all the blocks in a Log Cabin quilt. The light and dark fabrics can be handled in different ways. In my Log Cabin quilts, I plan fabric arrangements for two sets of blocks that are then set in a checkerboard fashion to make the overall design. The outside fabric on one block is never the same as on the block next to it. This way, the complicated look of a scrap quilt is preserved, but the planning is fairly simple.

The first design in this section, the Log Cabin wall quilt, is a good example of this fabric arrangement. It is made of two sets of 5" Log Cabin blocks; each with two light fabrics, two dark, and one accent. In total, four lights, four darks, and one accent, or nine different fabrics are needed to complete the design as pictured. Within each group of lights or darks, there should be little change in basic color, but good variation of visual texture. (See Figure 33.)

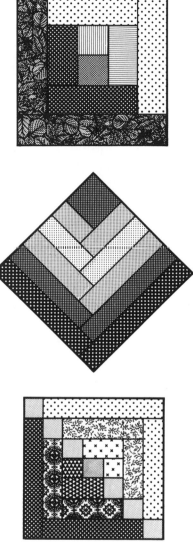

Figure 33. Choosing fabric for a "5" Log Cabin block

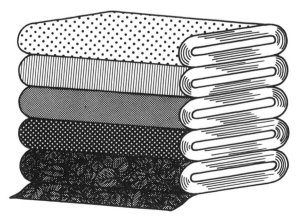

Piecing

The piecing of any wall quilt to be mounted on a wooden stretcher bar frame should be as flat and even as possible. Little puckers and slightly wavy seam lines that would not be important if the piece were to be quilted, become glaring mistakes when it is "stretched" unquilted. The Log Cabin and Log Cabin with a Chain wall quilt designs are especially good for mounting unquilted because all the pieces are cut on the straight grain of fabric. The only sewing involved is straight seams on the sewing machine.

Machine-pieced patchwork "stretches" better than hand-pieced work because the seams are stronger and the lines cleaner. Using templates for Log Cabin blocks, rather than the popular strip methods, helps produce flat, precise, stretchable patchwork.

Before cutting and piecing the blocks for your Log Cabin wall quilt, construct a sample block of the design to make sure you understand the piecing order and color placement. Cut the pieces precisely and sew exact 1/4" seams. Start with the center accent square as #1 in the piecing order and work outward. Sew the #2 piece to #1. Press the seam away from the center square. Then sew the #3 piece to the #1-#2 unit, and so on. Pay close attention to the piecing diagram provided with the pattern.

When the sample block is satisfactorily completed, cut the pieces for one set of Log Cabin blocks that are all alike (e.g. all eight Block I's for the Log Cabin wall quilt). All these blocks can be pieced at one time. Stack the cut pieces in their piecing order with the #1 center square on top, the #2 piece just below it, and so on. Chain piece (see "Machine Piecing" on page 11) all the #3 pieces to the first units. Clip, press and continue sewing following the piecing order. Because you are working on all the blocks simultaneously, they will all be completed at the same time. It really goes very quickly.

Cut and piece extra blocks for matching pillows at the same time you do them for your wall quilt.

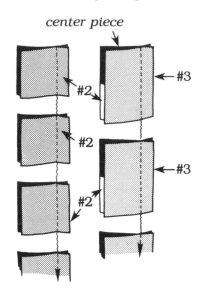

Figure 34. Chain piecing

Figure 35. Log Cabin designs with different arrangements of lights and darks.

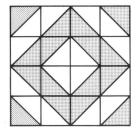 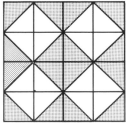 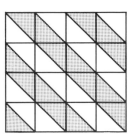 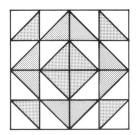

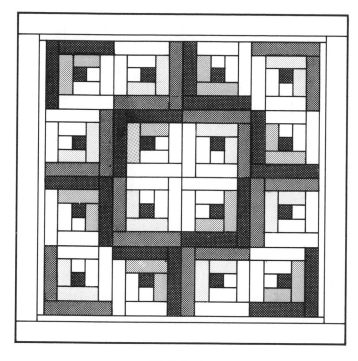

Wall Quilt

Log Cabin

5" Unit Blocks

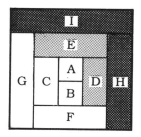

Block I

Block II

— Accent Color

Piecing Sequence

Color:

The two sets of Log Cabin blocks in this pattern have the same pattern pieces, but different fabrics. Each block contains a center square of the solid accent color plus two light-colored prints and two dark ones (see unit block illustration on this page). According to the illustration and placement in the design, assign each of your fabrics a number code: the first light fabric becomes L1 and the first dark fabric becomes D1, etc. Each pattern piece tells how many pieces to cut of each fabric according to its code.

Dimensions: 26" x 26"

Measurements for pattern pieces and borders include 1/4" seam allowances.

Materials: 45"-wide yardage
1/4 yd. solid accent color for centers and first border
1/8 yd. each of 4 dark prints (D1, D2, D3, D4)
1/8 yd. each of 4 light prints (L1, L2, L3, L4)
3/4 yd. solid color for outside border
1 yd. unbleached muslin for lining
4 - 26" wooden stretcher bars
   or
1 - 26" dowel or flat stick, thin batting, and binding to finish as a quilted hanging

Directions:
1. Cut and sew eight of Block I and eight of Block II. Use the chain piecing method described on page 26.
2. Place the sixteen completed blocks together alternately, in a checkerboard fashion. Try different arrangements of light and dark (Figure 35). Decide on your favorite arrangement and sew the blocks together with 1/4" seams. Make rows of blocks first, then sew the rows together. (See "Sets" on page 13.)
3. Read the section on "Finishing" on page 16 before going on. Choose the best method for finishing your piece.
4. Cut the border strips and sew them to the pieced section with straight sewn corners. (See Figure 10 for piecing order and "Borders" on page 14.)

INSIDE BORDER, accent color:
Cut two 1" x 20 1/2" strips.
Cut two 1" x 21 1/2" strips.

5. Finish using one of the methods outlined on page 16.

For a wall quilt mounted on a stretcher bar frame:
OUTSIDE BORDER, solid color:
Cut two 5" x 21 1/2" strips.
Cut two 5" x 30 1/2" strips.

For a wall quilt to be quilted and hung with a rod pocket and dowel:
OUTSIDE BORDER, solid color:
Cut two 3' x 21 1/2" strips.
Cut two 3" x 26 1/2" strips.

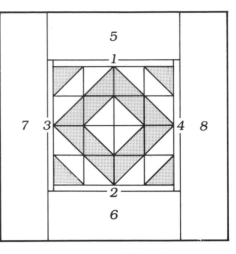

Piecing sequence of borders.

Log Cabin Pattern Sheet

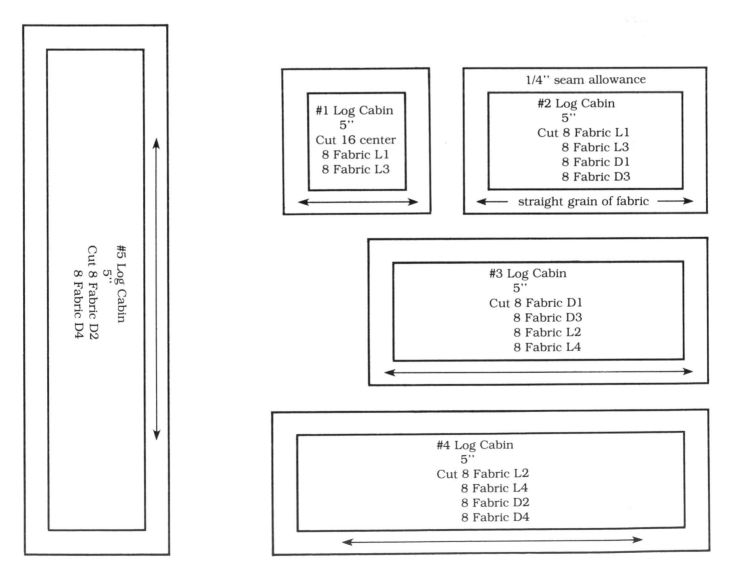

#5 Log Cabin
5"
Cut 8 Fabric D2
8 Fabric D4

#1 Log Cabin
5"
Cut 16 center
8 Fabric L1
8 Fabric L3

1/4" seam allowance

#2 Log Cabin
5"
Cut 8 Fabric L1
8 Fabric L3
8 Fabric D1
8 Fabric D3

straight grain of fabric

#3 Log Cabin
5"
Cut 8 Fabric D1
8 Fabric D3
8 Fabric L2
8 Fabric L4

#4 Log Cabin
5"
Cut 8 Fabric L2
8 Fabric L4
8 Fabric D2
8 Fabric D4

Wall Quilt

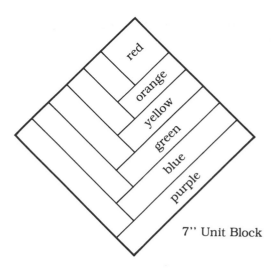

7" Unit Block

Rainbow Log Cabin

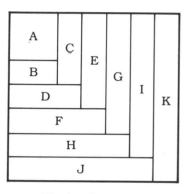

Piecing Sequence

Color:

The Rainbow Log Cabin has six rainbow colors in the unit blocks, and unbleached muslin is used for the background set pieces. The example pictured on page 38 is mounted unquilted on a wooden stretcher bar frame. Sometimes diagonal sets don't "stretch" well, but here the piecing is flat and it works nicely.

Dimensions: 12" x 32"

Measurements for borders and pattern pieces include 1/4" seam allowances.

Materials: 45"-wide yardage

1/8 yd. each of solid red, orange, yellow, green, blue and purple for unit blocks

1/2 yd. unbleached muslin for background and border

5/8 yd. unbleached muslin for lining

2 - 12" wooden stretcher bars

2 - 32" wooden stretcher bars
or

1 - 12" dowel or flat stick, thin batting and binding to finish as a quilted hanging

Directions:

1. Cut and piece three Rainbow Log Cabin blocks. Starting with the red corner square, follow the piecing sequence, and sew each piece in the order shown.

2. Cut four each of #8 and #9 set pieces.

3. Sew the blocks and set pieces together as pictured. (See Sets on page 13.)

4. Read the section on "Finishing" on page 16, then choose the best method for finishing your project.

5. Cut the border strips and sew them to the pieced section with straight-sewn corners. See "Borders" on page 14.

For a wall quilt to be mounted on a stretcher bar frame:

Cut two 4" x 30" strips.

Cut two 4" x 17 1/2" strips.

For a quilted piece hung with a rod pocket and dowel:

Cut two 1 1/2" x 30" strips.

Cut two 1 1/2" x 12 1/2" strips.

6. Finish by one of the methods outlined on page 16.

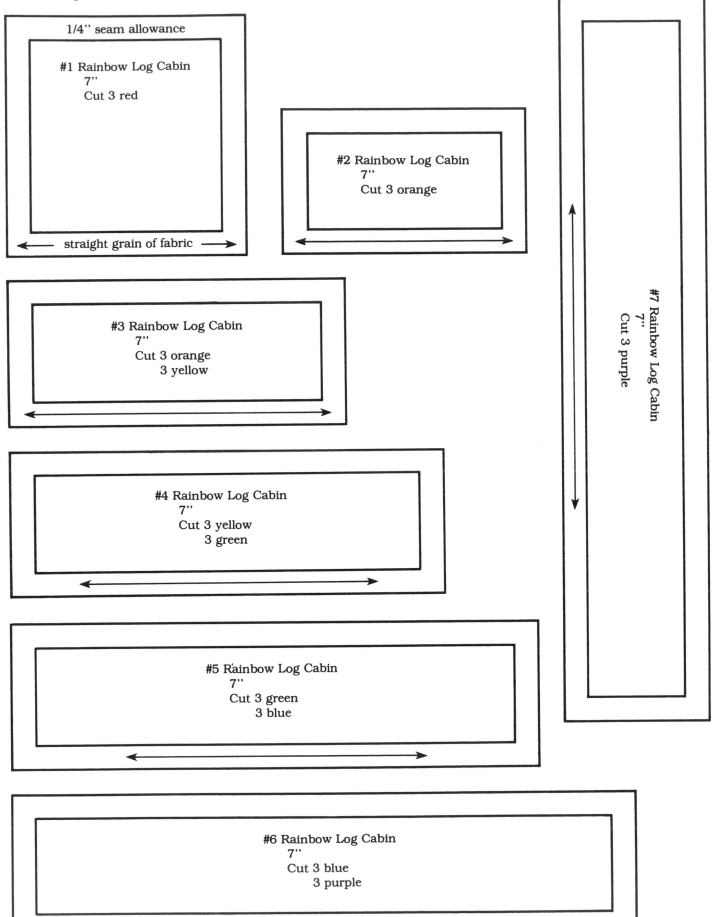

1/4" seam allowance

#1 Rainbow Log Cabin
7"
Cut 3 red

← straight grain of fabric →

#2 Rainbow Log Cabin
7"
Cut 3 orange

#3 Rainbow Log Cabin
7"
Cut 3 orange
3 yellow

#4 Rainbow Log Cabin
7"
Cut 3 yellow
3 green

#5 Rainbow Log Cabin
7"
Cut 3 green
3 blue

#6 Rainbow Log Cabin
7"
Cut 3 blue
3 purple

#7 Rainbow Log Cabin
7"
Cut 3 purple

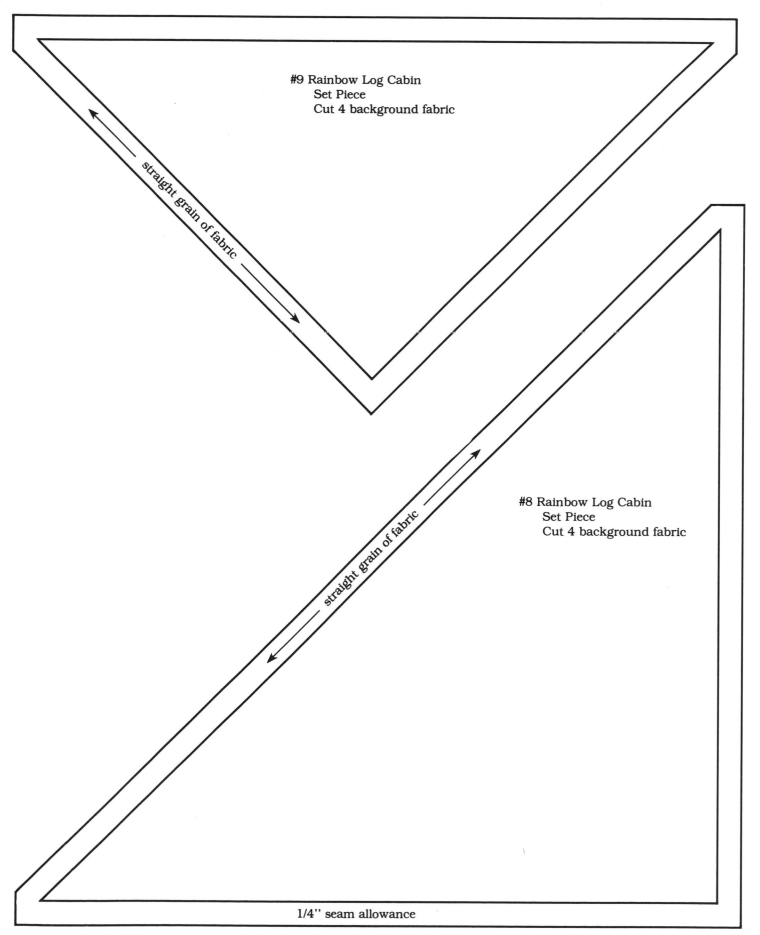

#9 Rainbow Log Cabin
Set Piece
Cut 4 background fabric

straight grain of fabric

#8 Rainbow Log Cabin
Set Piece
Cut 4 background fabric

straight grain of fabric

1/4'' seam allowance

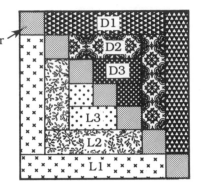

Accent Color

Block I

Log Cabin with a Chain

7" Unit Blocks

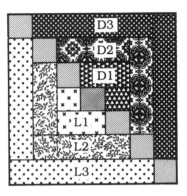

Block II

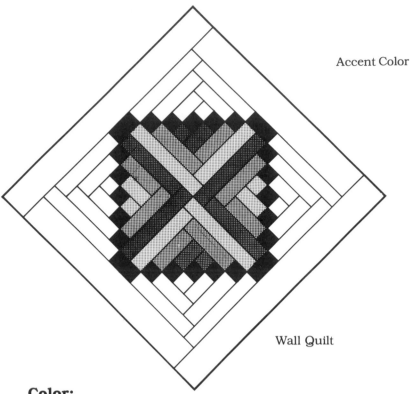

Wall Quilt

Color:

The Log Cabin with a Chain is an old-fashioned variation of the traditional Log Cabin pattern. The unit block is composed of light, medium and dark fabrics. The light half has three light-colored prints, the dark half has three dark-colored prints, and the chain of accent squares is usually a medium or dark solid.

According to the illustration and placement in the design, assign each of your fabrics a number code: the first light fabric becomes L1 and the first dark becomes D1, and so on. Notice that the same fabrics are used in Blocks I and II but in reversed order. (Block I has L1 and D1 on the outside and Block II has L3 and D3 on the outside.) Each pattern piece on page 33 tells how many pieces to cut of each fabric according to its code.

Dimensions: 18" x 18"

Measurements for pattern pieces and borders include 1/4" seam allowances.

Materials: 45"-wide yardage
1/8 yd. solid accent color for "chains"
1/8 yd. each of three dark prints (D1, D2, D3)
1/8 yd. each of three light prints (L1, L2, L3)
3/4 yd. solid color for outside border
3/4 yd. unbleached muslin for lining
4 - 18" wooden stretcher bars
   or
1 - 18" dowel, thin batting, and binding to
   finish as a quilted hanging

Piecing Sequence

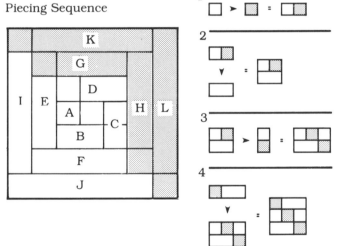

Directions:
1. Cut and piece two of Block I and two of Block II. Begin by sewing one accent square to a light square. Sew this unit to the #2 light piece. Now, sew one accent square to each dark strip and piece the strips in order as shown in the "Piecing Sequence."
2. Set the four blocks together. As with the Log Cabin wall quilt, there are several possible arrangements of light and dark, so try different placements before sewing the blocks together.
3. Read the section on "Finishing" on page 16. Choose the best method for finishing your piece.

4. Cut the border strips and sew them to the pieced sections with straight-sewn corners. See "Borders" on page 14.

For a wall quilt mounted on a stretcher bar frame:

    Cut two 5" x 14 1/2" strips.
    Cut two 5" x 24" strips.

For a piece to be quilted and hung with rod pocket and dowel:

    Cut two 2 1/2" x 14 1/2" strips.
    Cut two 2 1/2" x 18 1/2" strips.

5. Finish using one of the methods outlined on page 16.

Log Cabin with a Chain Pattern Sheet

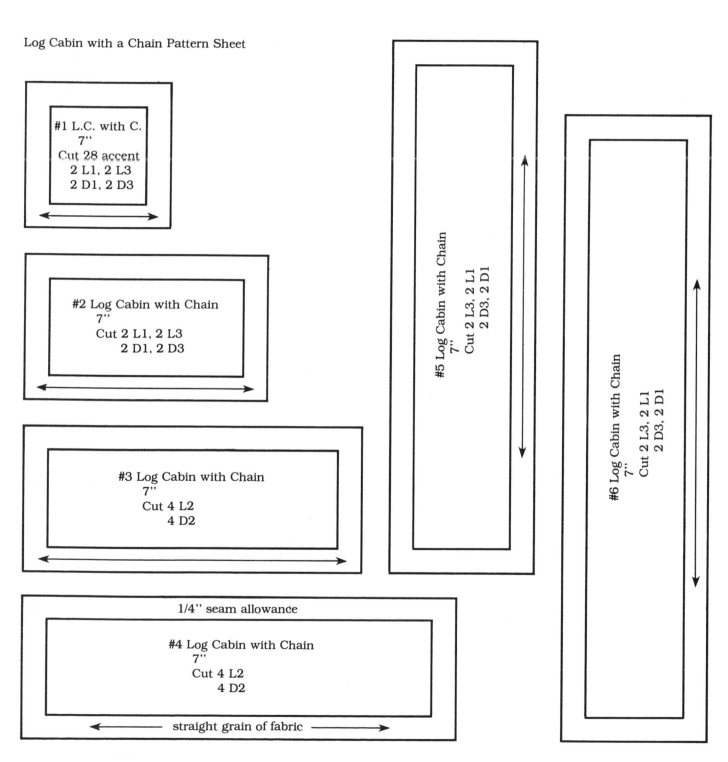

Wall Quilt

12" Unit Block

Pineapple

Piecing Diagram

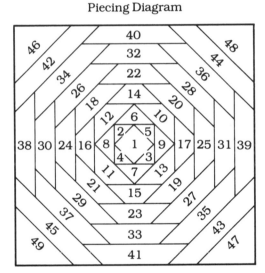

Color:

The Pineapple block is versatile and dynamic. Make a small wall quilt or pillow from one block or a larger hanging or quilt from four or more blocks. A Log Cabin variation, the Pineapple has an accent color for the center. The rest of the pieces are arranged in a strong light-and-dark pattern consisting of many fabrics.

Dimensions: 28" x 28"

Measurements for borders and pattern pieces include 1/4" seam allowances.

Materials: 45"-wide fabric
1/8 yd. or scraps of accent color for centers
1/2 yd. total of 3 to 5 different dark prints
1/2 yd. total of 3 to 5 different light prints
3/4 yd. border fabric
1 yd. unbleached muslin for lining
4 - 28" wooden stretcher bars
    or
1 - 28" dowel or flat stick, thin batting and
    binding to finish as a quilted hanging

Directions:

1. Cut and piece four Pineapple blocks, two of one fabric arrangement and two of another. (Read the section on fabric choice for Log Cabins on page 25.) Start piecing this design in the center and build out. The numbers in the piecing diagram indicate the sewing order.
2. Set the four blocks together.
3. Read the section on "Finishing" on page 16. Choose the best method for finishing your piece. The example pictured on page 37 has been quilted and mounted on a wooden stretcher bar frame.

34

4. Cut border strips and sew them to the pieced section with straight sewn corners. (See "Borders" on page 14.)

For a wall quilt mounted on a stretcher bar frame:

Cut two 5" x 24 1/2" strips

Cut two 5" x 34" strips

For a wall quilt to be finished as a quilt and hung with a rod pocket and dowel:

Cut two 2 1/2" x 24 1/2" strips.

Cut two 2 1/2" x 28 1/2" strips.

5. Finish, using one of the methods outlined on page 16.

Pineapple Pattern Sheet

Note: Numbers on each pattern piece indicate how many pieces to cut for one unit block: four blocks are required to make the wall quilt as pictured on page 34.

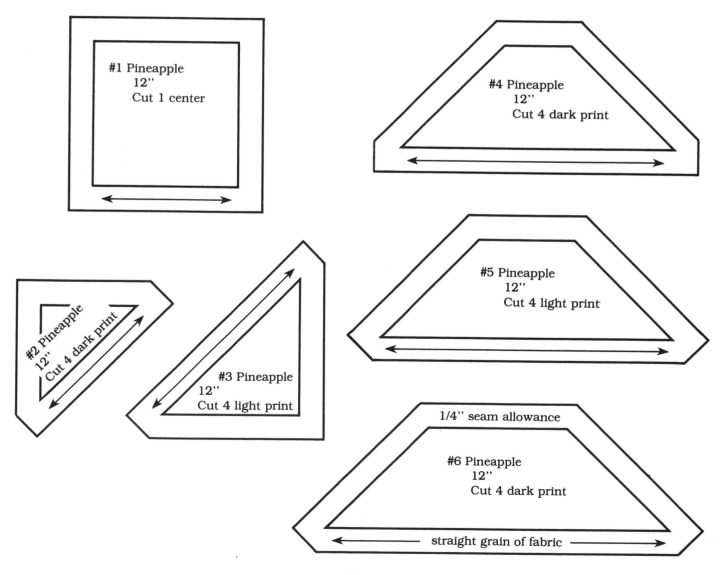

#1 Pineapple 12" Cut 1 center

#2 Pineapple 12" Cut 4 dark print

#3 Pineapple 12" Cut 4 light print

#4 Pineapple 12" Cut 4 dark print

#5 Pineapple 12" Cut 4 light print

1/4" seam allowance

#6 Pineapple 12" Cut 4 dark print

straight grain of fabric

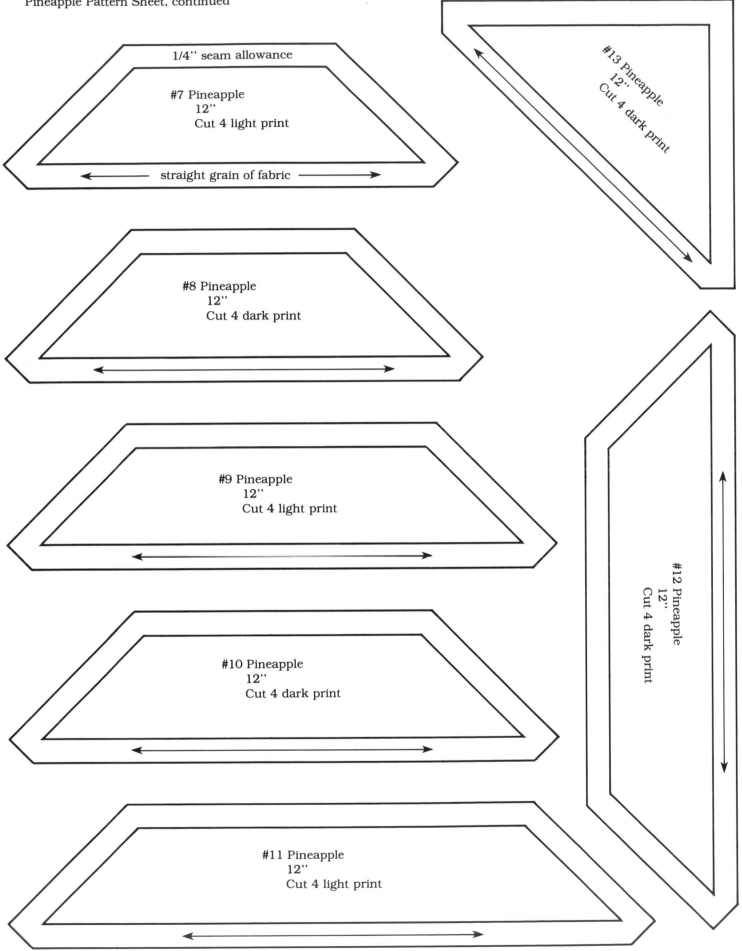

1/4'' seam allowance

#7 Pineapple
12''
Cut 4 light print

straight grain of fabric

#13 Pineapple
12''
Cut 4 dark print

#8 Pineapple
12''
Cut 4 dark print

#9 Pineapple
12''
Cut 4 light print

#12 Pineapple
12''
Cut 4 dark print

#10 Pineapple
12''
Cut 4 dark print

#11 Pineapple
12''
Cut 4 light print

Right: Pineapple wall quilt (28" x 28") with Log Cabin pillows. The wall quilt was pieced and quilted, then mounted on a wooden stretcher bar frame.

Below: This Log Cabin with a Chain wall quilt (14" x 14") was mounted unquilted on a wooden stretcher bar frame. The pieced pillow and Sunshine and Shadow quilt in the basket are by Pam Boag.

Below Right: The Log Cabin wall quilt (26" x 26") was mounted unquilted on stretcher bars. The Flying Geese I quilt (shown on chair) is a variation of the design, made by Nancy Martin.

Left: Rainbow Log Cabin wall quilt (12" x 32") is mounted unquilted on a wooden stretcher bar frame. The rainbow Sunshine and Shadow crib quilt and the Flying Geese II pillow with the black background show variations on the rainbow color theme.

Below: The Flying Geese I wall quilt (45" x 54") has been quilted and hung using the rod-pocket-and-dowel method.

Below Left: Cool solid colors have been used in the Flying Geese I wall quilt by Gretchen Engel and the Grandmother's Dream by Nancy Martin.

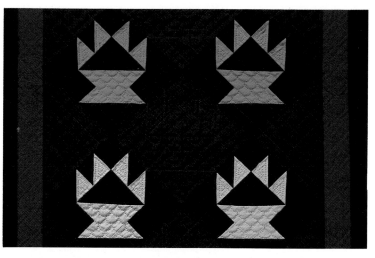

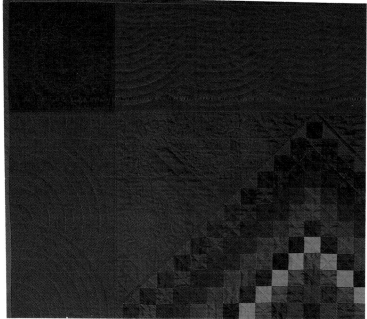

Above: Baskets wall quilt (26" x 51 1/2"), pieced by the author and quilted by Nancy Dice, is hung with a rod pocket and dowel.

Top Right: Detail of Nancy Dice's quilting on the Baskets wall quilt.

Middle Right: Grandmother's Dream wall quilt shows the detail of Feather Plume, Feather Wreath and Ocean Waves quilting designs by Nancy Dice.

Bottom Right: Grandmother's Dream wall quilt (55" x 55"), pieced by the author and quilted by Nancy Dice, is hung using the rod-pocket-and-dowel method. Also shown are Pine Tree pillows and an antique quilt courtesy of Sharon Yenter.

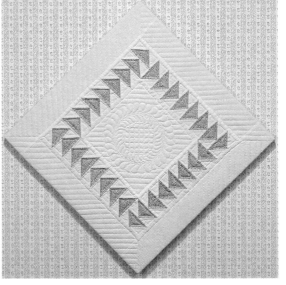

Top: This Sunshine and Shadow design variation called Trip Around the World (32'' x 32'') was pieced and mounted unquilted on a wooden stretcher bar frame. Notice the variety of visual texture in the prints used, and how they build from light to medium to dark tones.

Left: The Pine Tree wall quilt (18 1/4'' x 42 3/4'') was quilted and hung with a rod pocket and dowel. Also shown are Pineapple and Pine Tree pillows.

Above: The Flying Geese II wall quilt (20'' x 20'') features the Feather Wreath quilting motif found on page 53.

Notes on Sunshine and Shadow Designs

Tied to the land and its rhythms by strict religious beliefs and rigid communal order, the women of the Amish sect of Pennsylvania in the early 1900's made their quilts of all solid-colored fabrics in simple geometric designs. In the quilts they called Sunshine and Shadow, rows of small squares alternated light and dark colors to create overall designs. The name refers to Scripture; after the darkness will come the light. The concept appeals to me. It speaks of life's rhythms and of faith and hope. Some quilters today call all of these quilts and their variations Trip Around the World. I prefer to call the whole group by the Amish term, Sunshine and Shadow, and designate the design variations by specific names.

In a Streak of Lightning, the simplest of the Sunshine and Shadow designs, the colored rows run on the diagonal across the quilt's surface. In Trip Around the World, the colored rows form concentric diamonds or squares "on point." Grandmother's Dream is like Trip Around the World, but is tipped on its side and the final outside row is made not of squares, but of triangles. These designs can be square as presented here, or rectangular. The colored rows can form zigzags or multiple "around the worlds." The squares can be large or small; the colors can be any you choose. You may wish to vary the designs here to better fit a space or color theme.

Color and Fabric Choice

First, choose a color theme. Study the picture of the Sunshine and Shadow, Trip Around the World wall quilt.

The best way I know to pick fabrics is to first get out all the fabric pieces in your home collection that might fit the color theme. Then play—arrange the pieces in different orders from light to medium to dark, and back again. Try to imagine what they will look like in your quilt design. Squint at the fabrics: light, medium and dark tones become very obvious this way. Some fabrics won't work at all, so they go back on the shelf. If you don't feel you have enough for your quilt, take the usable pieces with you to the fabric store and continue playing with fabric progressions until a satisfactory effect is achieved. In a Sunshine and Shadow design, the color order can be repeated several times, reversed, or changed at different parts of the design.

Keep in mind that gradual progression from light to dark gives a soft look to the quilt, as does including some larger prints in fabric groupings. Sharply contrasting fabrics placed next to each other create a hard line. This is desirable at some places in the design, but should not be overused. Linear prints, stripes and checks are harder to cut and sew than all-over designs. Unless one is willing to take the special care involved in their use, they are better left out entirely.

Working with solid colors is similar to working with prints in that gradual progressions from light to dark and careful

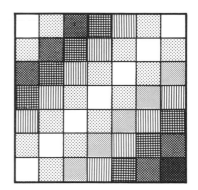

Streak of Lightning

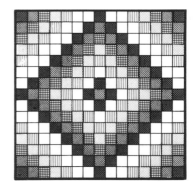

Trip Around the World

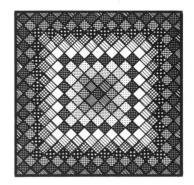

Grandmother's Dream

placement of sharp contrasts are still desirable. A somewhat limiting color theme is absolutely essential to help you zero in on certain color groups. Study color photographs of quilts that appeal to you and write down the color progressions used. Study a color wheel for ideas. Pay attention to warm (yellow undertone) and cool (blue undertone) colors. A theme limited to warm or cool colors can work nicely, although mixing the two can set up startling and delightful color combinations (as we often see in Amish solid-color quilts).

Once a color theme for solids is established, again play with the fabrics until you arrive at a set of pleasing color progressions. Seven different fabrics is a good number to start with and is good for small projects. Large quilt projects need at least twelve to fifteen colors.

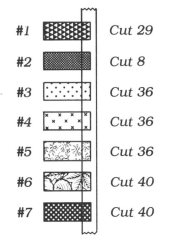

Figure 36. Example of color key

Color Key

When you have chosen fabrics and decided on a progression, make a color key to help you remember the sequence of the colors. Assign each fabric a number that corresponds to its placement in the Sunshine and Shadow design (see numbered charts with the Sunshine and Shadow designs). Most fabrics will be used more than once, but each needs only one number for the color key. Cut a small piece of each fabric. Arrange the swatches in sequence and tape them to a piece of paper. Next to each one, write the assigned number and the amount of squares to be cut. (See Figure 36.) Keep your color key handy while you are cutting and sewing.

Cutting

Use a paper template and cut four layers at a time. Take care to align each layer so all pieces will be cut on the straight grain of fabric. Cut in multiples of four even if it means cutting a few extra squares. If the design calls for fourteen squares, cut sixteen (4 cuts x 4 layers = 16 squares). If 22 squares are needed, cut twenty four (4 x 6 = 24) and so on. Not having to refold the fabric to cut odd numbers saves more time than the extra squares are worth. Arrange the cut squares in piles in numerical order.

Piecing

The piecing technique I have evolved for Sunshine and Shadow designs is just chain piecing taken a step further. Sections are chain pieced as units, then set together to make the larger overall design. Chain piecing keeps the individual rows in order. Sewing goes very quickly, involves little or no pinning, and no ironing until the very end. For clarity, I have described the method in the directions for the Sunshine and Shadow, Trip Around the World wall quilt. Though it is a very logical proceeding, I find it more easily understood if you have cut pieces and a sewing machine in front of you. To most of my students, understanding comes with a "flash and a grin" when they suddenly see the logic and simplicity of this method. I think you will enjoy it too. Read the instructions over a few times before you begin, then take it one step at a time.

Wall Quilt

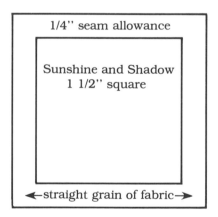

Design Units

Sunshine and Shadow
Trip Around the World

Pattern Piece

1/4" seam allowance

Sunshine and Shadow
1 1/2" square

←straight grain of fabric→

Color:

Choose seven fabrics ranging from light to medium to dark tones. Prints or solids can be used. (See "Color and Fabric Choice" on page 41.) If you wish to follow this design exactly, choose three light, two medium and two dark prints. For help, study the color picture of the Trip Around the World wall quilt on page 40. Assign each fabric a number according to its placement in the design (see Figure 26) and make a color key to help guide your cutting and sewing. (See Color Key on page 42.)

Dimensions: 32" x 32"

Measurements for borders and pattern pieces include 1/4" seam allowances.

Materials: 45"-wide yardage
1/4 yd. each of seven different fabrics ranging from light to medium to dark tones (there will be enough left over to make pillow tops)
7/8 yd. dark solid for borders
1 1/8 yds. unbleached muslin for lining
4 - 32" wooden stretcher bars
      or
1 - 32" dowel or flat stick, thin batting, and binding to finish as a quilted hanging

Directions:

1. Cut out the number of fabric squares indicated on the color key. (See figure 38 and "Cutting" on page 42.)

2. Piece four Unit C. To start, have the cut squares, color key, and numbered line drawing (Figure 37) at the sewing machine. You will be dealing with bands of color that run diagonally in the design, and construction rows A through G that run horizontally. The first color band has one square of color #3, which is located at the upper left of design Unit C. The second color band has two squares of color #4.

To start the first construction Row A, sew one #4 square to the #3 square. (The other #4 square will begin Row B.) The third color band contains three #5 squares. Chain piece a #5 square to each Row A and Row B. (The third #5 square will begin Row C.) The fourth color band has four #1 squares. Chain piece one of these to each of the three preceding rows. (The fourth #1 square begins Row D.) (See Figure 39.)

Do not cut the threads (chains) between the construction rows. Leaving them attached will keep the rows in order as the piecing continues. *Do not iron at this time.*

Each new color band adds one square to each of the previous construction rows and begins a new one. Continue piecing in this manner until construction Row A is seven squares long. At this point, construction rows A through G will all have been started. Keep Row A attached to the incomplete rows, but don't sew any more squares to it. Add the next color band beginning with Row B and ending with Row G. As each construction row reaches seven squares long, stop adding squares to it. Keep adding color bands. The number of squares in each band will now decrease by one each time. (The last color band, like the first, has only one square.) Add color bands until all the construction rows are complete.

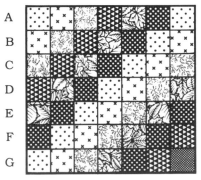

The rows sewn together look like this.

Figure 37.

A

Make 1 | 1 |

C

B	2		3	4	5	1	6	7	3
	3		4	5	1	6	7	3	4
	4		5	1	6	7	3	4	5
	5		1	6	7	3	4	5	6
	1		6	7	3	4	5	6	7
	6		7	3	4	5	6	7	1
	7		3	4	5	6	7	1	2

Make 4   Make 4

Figure 38.

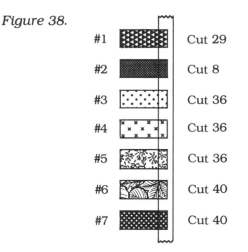

#1 Cut 29
#2 Cut 8
#3 Cut 36
#4 Cut 36
#5 Cut 36
#6 Cut 40
#7 Cut 40

Figure 39.

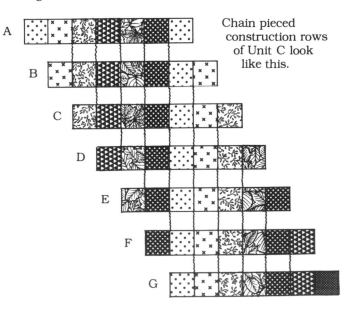

Chain pieced construction rows of Unit C look like this.

44

To sew the completed construction rows together, cut rows A and B free of the others. Match the ends (they've been offset by one square until now) and sew the rows together with a 1/4" seam allowance. On this first long seam, the seam allowances on top should all be finger pressed towards you; those underneath, away from you. All the seams will be "opposing" (see page 12) and neatly matched corners will result. Pin only if you feel you need to. Wait to iron until all the units are sewn together and you are ready to add borders. When the third row (Row C) is added, the seam allowances on top will be finger pressed away from you; those underneath, towards you. The direction of the seam allowances will alternate row by row. It is important that the seam allowances on all four Unit C be pressed in exactly the same order (eg. start with the seam allowances on top pressed towards you on the first row). Then, when all the units are set together, the seam allowances will meet in proper "opposition" all the way around.

Figure 40.

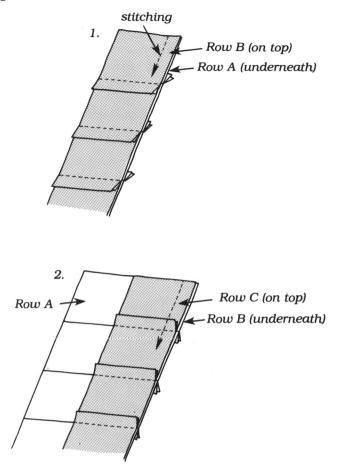

3. Piece four Unit B. Chain piecing these identical units is an efficient use of time and thread. Begin by chaining four #3 squares to four #2 squares as pictured. Do not cut the chains. Add one #4 square to each of the four rows and so on until each row is seven squares long. Cut the "chains" to separate the rows.

4. Set the A, B, and C units together as pictured in Figure 42.

5. Press the pieced section thoroughly, first on the back then on the front.

Figure 41.

| 2 | 3 | 4 | 5 | 1 | 6 | 7 |

Chain pieced B units look like this.

6. Read the section on "Finishing" on page 16. Choose the best method for finishing your piece. The Trip Around the World wall quilt pictured on page 40 was pieced and mounted unquilted, on a wooden stretcher bar frame.

7. Cut border strips and sew them to the pieced section with straight-sewn corners. (See "Borders" on page 14).

For a wall quilt mounted on a stretcher bar frame:

Cut two 8" x 23" strips.
Cut two 8" x 38" strips.

For a wall quilt to be finished as a quilt and hung with a rod pocket and dowel:

Cut two 5" x 23" strips.
Cut two 5" x 32 1/2" strips.

8. Finish by one of the methods outlined on page 16.

Figure 42.

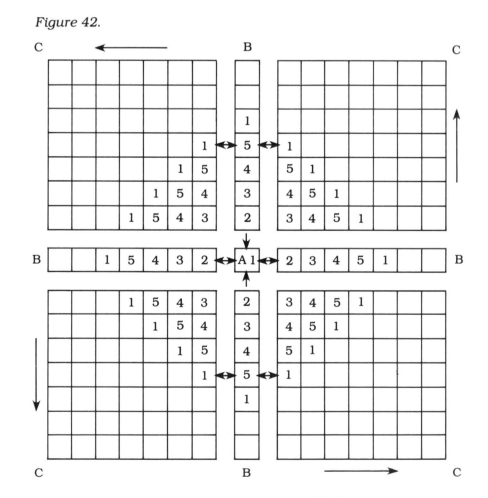

The design units for Trip Around the World are set together like this.

Wall Quilt

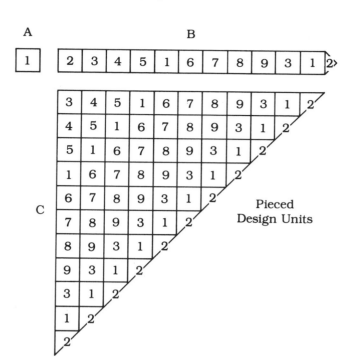

A   B

C   Pieced Design Units

Sunshine and Shadow Grandmother's Dream

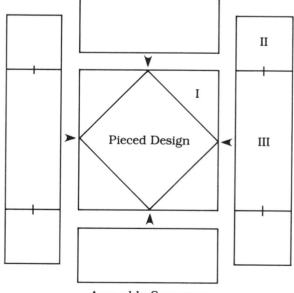

Assembly Sequence

Color:

The Grandmother's Dream example on page 39 is made of 100% cotton Amish-style solid-color fabrics. For help with selecting fabrics for solid-color Sunshine and Shadow designs, turn to page 41. Nine colors are needed to make the design as pictured here. Choose your own color combination or follow the pattern as shown. Nancy Dice's quilting motifs (see page 51) add wonderful texture to the large unpieced areas of the wall quilt.

Dimensions: 55" x 55"

Measurements for borders and pattern pieces include 1/4" seam allowances.

Materials: 45"-wide yardage

1 1/4 yds. fabric #1, navy for small squares, large Triangle I and large corner Square II.

1/4 yd. fabric #2, purple for pattern pieces, #1, #2 and #3

1/4 yd. fabric #3, dark green

1/8 yd. fabric #4, medium green

1/8 yd. fabric #5, light green

1 yd. fabric #6, blue-gray for small squares and binding

1/4 yd. fabric #7, pink

1 3/8 yd. fabric #8, dark pink for small squares and Borders (III)

1/4 yd. fabric #9, brown

3 1/8 yd. muslin, print or solid for backing

1 - 55" dowel or flat stick, thin batting and binding to finish as a quilted hanging.

Grandmother's Dream Pattern Sheet

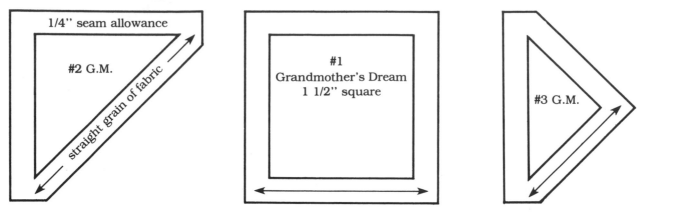

Directions:

1. Read cutting for Sunshine and Shadow designs on page 42. Cut the small fabric squares and triangles according to the amounts indicated on the Color Key (Figure 43).

2. Piece four C units. See Figure 44 and step 2 of directions for the Sunshine and Shadow wall quilt on page 44.

Figure 44. Unit C
Chain pieced rows in Unit C look like this.

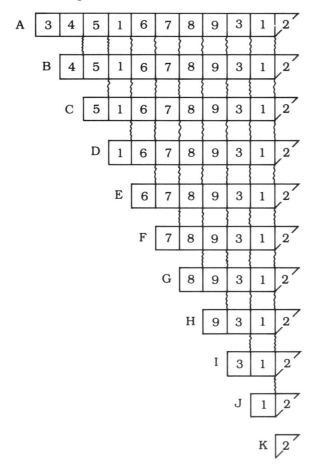

Figure 43. Color key

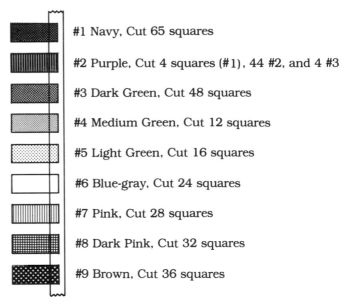

#1 Navy, Cut 65 squares

#2 Purple, Cut 4 squares (#1), 44 #2, and 4 #3

#3 Dark Green, Cut 48 squares

#4 Medium Green, Cut 12 squares

#5 Light Green, Cut 16 squares

#6 Blue-gray, Cut 24 squares

#7 Pink, Cut 28 squares

#8 Dark Pink, Cut 32 squares

#9 Brown, Cut 36 squares

The rows sewn together look like this.

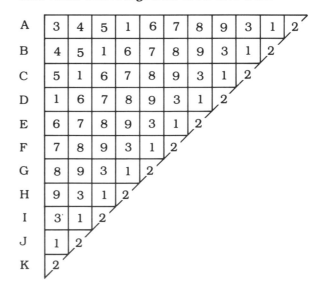

3. Piece four B units.

4. Set A, B and C units as pictured in Figure 46.

5. Press pieced section.

Figure 46.

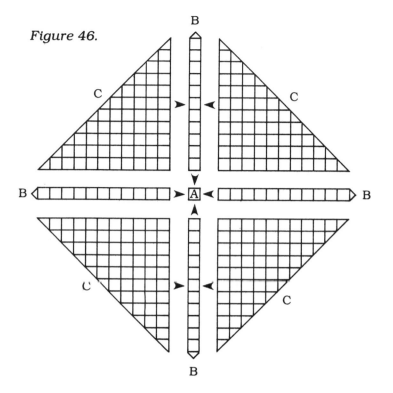

Figure 45. Chain pieced B units.

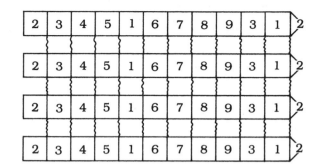

6. Triangle I: Mark two large squares directly on the navy fabric that measure 18 7/8" on each side. Divide each square in half on the diagonal and cut out the four resulting triangles (1/4" seam allowances are included). Sew them to the center pieced section according to the assembly sequence on page 47.

7. Corner Square II: Mark and cut four 10" squares (includes 1/4" seam allowance) of fabric #1, navy.

8. Border III: Cut four border strips to measure 10" x 36 1/2".

9. Set the parts together as pictured in the assembly sequence on page 47.

10. Make stencils, mark quilting lines, assemble quilt and hand quilt. See "Quilting" on page 22 for general directions and page 50 for specific quilting hints for this design.

11. Bind edges. (See "Binding" on page 23.)

12. Add rod pocket and hang with a dowel or flat stick as outlined on page 18.

Figure 47.

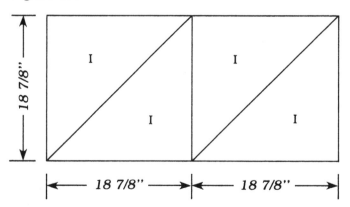

Notes on Marking the Quilting Designs for Grandmother's Dream

Chart A shows the all-over quilting pattern. Chart B is one half of the Feather Plume pattern for the corner triangles (I). Chart C is one half of the Feather Wreath pattern for the corner squares (II). Chart D is the stencil pattern for the Ocean Waves border design.

1. The center pieced diamond: Crosshatch the diamond diagonally with straight lines passing through every corner. These same lines extend into the corner triangles, up to the Feather Plumes, serving as background filler. In the triangles, these lines only go one direction. (See Chart A.)

2. The corner Feather Plumes: Only half of the pattern is given. Line up the stencil carefully with the seam lines. Flip the pattern over to mark the second half. Remember you can make minor adjustments in the quilting lines if you see that your stenciled lines are a little off or if the shapes are irregular in size. You will have to draw in every other quilting line by hand. Keep the individual "leaves" even. Quilt 1/4" in from the seam lines all around each large triangle.

3. The corner square Feather Wreaths: One half of the pattern is given. Remember to rotate the stencil to mark the second half; if it is flipped over, the wreath "leaves" will go in the opposite direction. Center the motifs in the corner squares according to the seam lines, not the edge of the fabric. Quilt 1/4" in from the seam lines around each corner square.

4. The outer borders: The stencil pattern (Chart D) for Ocean Waves is only part of the quilting pattern. You will need to pivot the stencil in order to mark the whole arc of the pattern on the border. Begin by marking the pivot points on the outside seam line of the border as indicated on Chart A. Put a pin through the stencil and a pivot point as indicated and swing the stencil to left. Subsequent "waves" extend from the previous wave to the seam line.

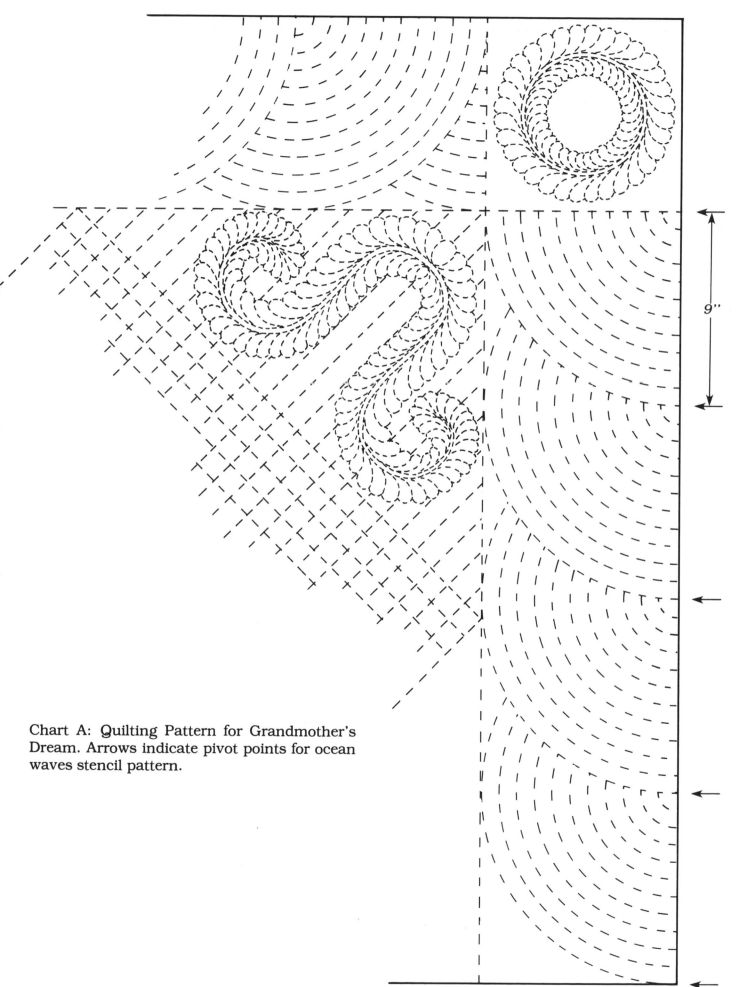

9"

Chart A: Quilting Pattern for Grandmother's
Dream. Arrows indicate pivot points for ocean
waves stencil pattern.

Center line

Seam line

Cut out →

Cut out →

Chart B: Feather Plume
Stencil and full-size quilting pattern for 1/2 of the design to be used for Grandmother's Dream wall quilt. Make stencil following instructions on page 20. Cut out shaded sections. When tracing design on fabric, draw inside of cut out areas; draw in dotted lines freehand. Flip stencil over for second half of pattern.

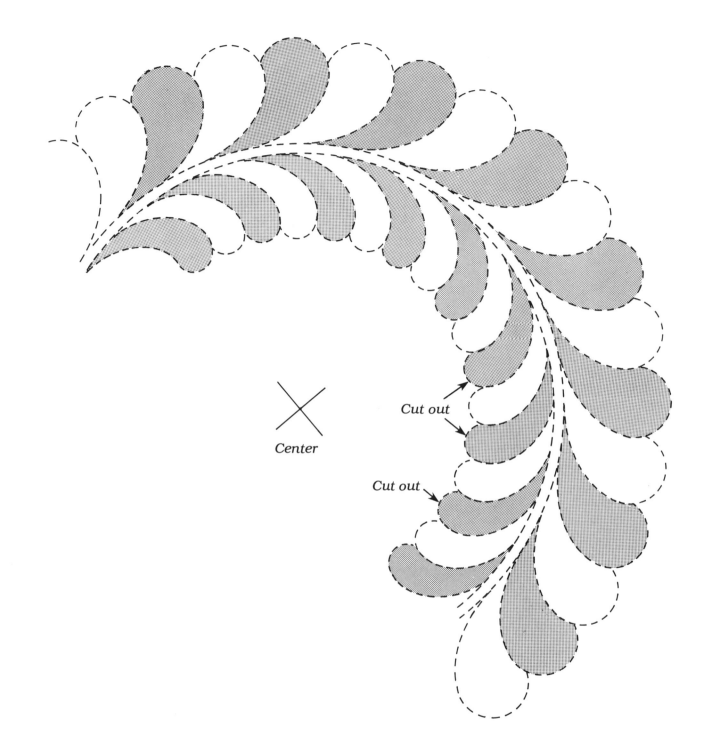

Center

Cut out

Cut out

Chart C: Feather Wreath
Stencil and full-size quilting pattern for 1/2 of design to be used in the corner squares of the Grandmother's Dream wall quilt and in the center square of Flying Geese II on page 67. Make stencil following instructions given on page 20. Cut out shaded sections. When tracing design on fabric, draw inside of cut out areas; draw dotted lines freehand. Rotate stencil for second half of pattern.

Cut out

Chart D: Ocean Waves
Stencil for quilting pattern for outer border of
Grandmother's Dream wall quilt. Make stencil
following instructions on page 20. Cut out the
shaded areas. When tracing design on fabric,
trace inside the cut outs. Rotate the stencil with
a pin at pivot points indicated on Chart A and
continue lines until they hit previously marked
quilting lines.

Triangle Designs

Wall Quilt

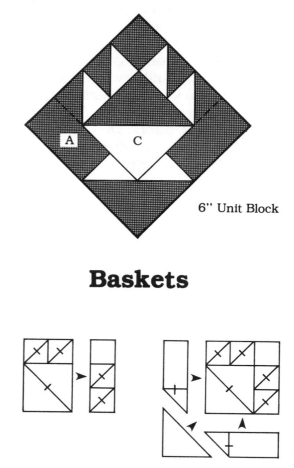

6" Unit Block

Baskets

Piecing Sequence

Color:

To achieve the Amish look for the Baskets wall quilt, choose all solid-color 100% cotton fabrics. Background colors can be dark brown, black, navy, wine or gray. Two tones of black were used in the example pictured on page 39; one for the background of the unit blocks and another for the set pieces. The brightly colored baskets can be one color or many. Experiment with different shades of pink, purple, turquoise, green and lavender. Put them all against the background fabric and squint at the different combinations. Which ones seem to glow and harmonize? Let the possibilities sit for a while and come back to them. Do they still work? Use the ones that you like best.

When using dark solid-colored fabrics, sew with a dark neutral thread like navy or black. In keeping with the Amish tradition, the Baskets quilt has been quilted with dark thread as well.

The diagonal set and many triangles in "Baskets" make it an inappropriate project for mounting unquilted on a stretcher bar frame,

unless the piecing is exceedingly flat. The example on page 39 was quilted by Nancy Dice. It was bound, and hung with a rod pocket and flat stick.

Dimensions: 26" x 51 1/2"

Measurements for borders and pattern pieces include 1/4" seam allowances.

Materials:

Fabric A, black for background of unit blocks and outside borders: 1 1/4" yds.

Fabric B, second black for set pieces: 1/2 yd.

Fabric C, one or many bright solids for baskets: 3/8 yd. total

Fabric D, bright solid for inside border and backing: 1 1/2 yds.

Batting, binding, thread and other materials to finish (See "Finishing" on page 16).

55

Directions:

1. Cut and piece 10 Basket unit blocks.
2. From fabric B, cut 5 of set piece #5, 8 of set piece #6, and 4 of piece #7.
3. Set unit blocks and set pieces together as pictured. (See "Sets" on page 13.)
4. Cut border strips and sew them together to form border units. (See "Borders" on page 14 and "Mitering" on page 15.)
  INSIDE BORDER, Fabric D:
    Cut two 2" x 26 1/2" strips.
    Cut two 2" x 52" strips.

OUTSIDE BORDER, Fabric A:
    Cut two 3 1/2" x 26 1/2" strips.
    Cut two 3 1/2" x 52" strips.

5. Add borders and miter corners.
6. Mark for quilting and hand quilt. Quilting suggestions are on the next few pages. For how to quilt, see "Quilting" on page 19. For other finishing techniques, see page 16.

Baskets Pattern Sheet

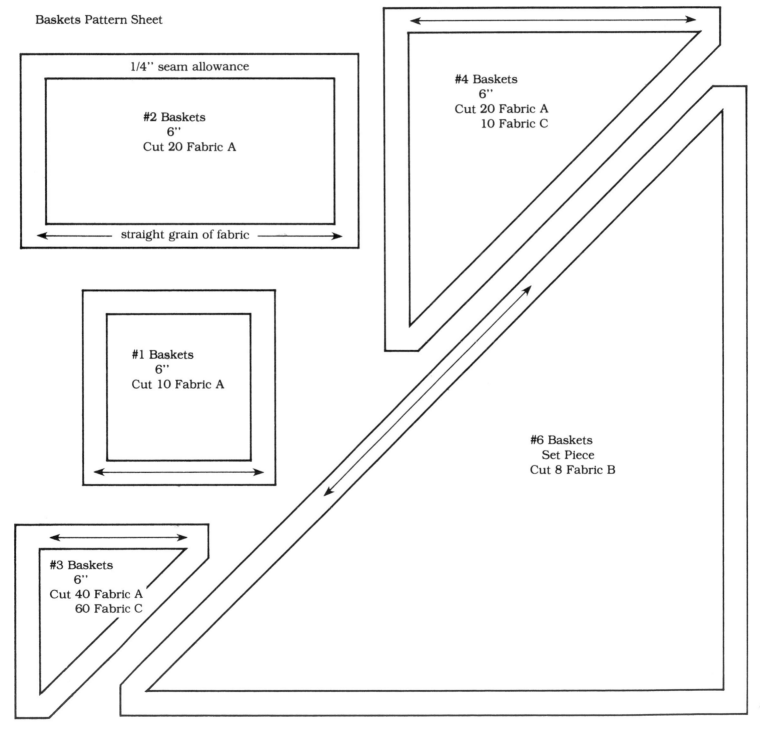

Baskets Pattern Sheet, continued.

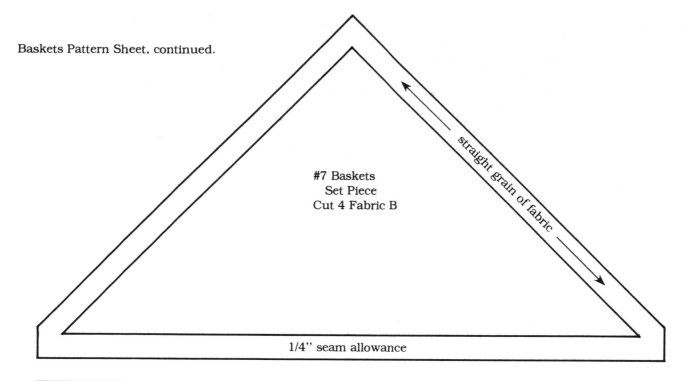

#7 Baskets
Set Piece
Cut 4 Fabric B

straight grain of fabric

1/4" seam allowance

#5 Baskets
Set Piece
Cut 5 Fabric B

(Also use for center of Flying Geese II pillow.)

Notes on Marking Quilting Design for Baskets

Chart A shows the overall quilting design for Baskets. Chart B shows the quilting motif for the inside border. Chart C is both the stencil pattern for the unpieced squares and a full-size quilting diagram for the pieced squares as well.

1. The unpieced squares: Position stencil (Chart C) and trace basket shape. Fill in the dotted lines using a ruler for the straight lines and half of your thimble for the small clam shell pattern in the bottom of the baskets.

2. The pieced basket squares: Fill in the dotted lines of the quilting pattern using a ruler and thimble as guides.

3. Draw in crosshatching background lines on all squares, and corner and side triangles using a ruler for a guide. Lines should be 3/4" apart.

Chart A: Quilting pattern for Baskets wall quilt.

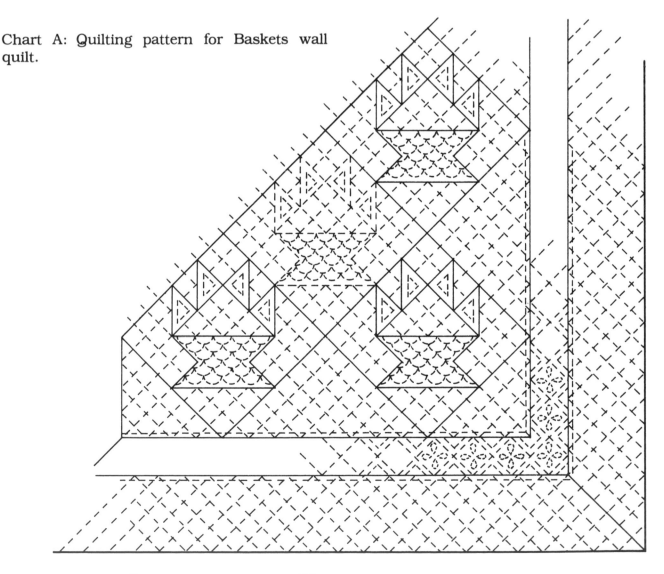

58

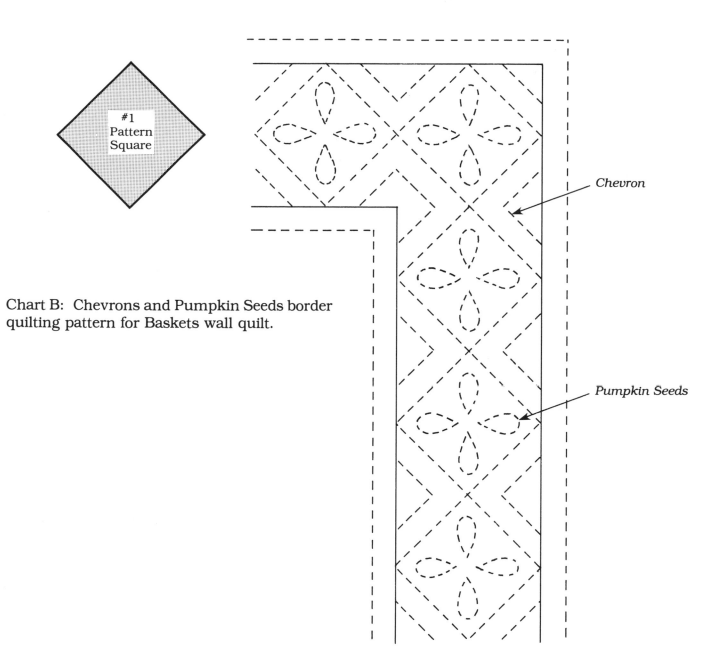

Chart B: Chevrons and Pumpkin Seeds border quilting pattern for Baskets wall quilt.

4. The inside border: Outline border with quilting 1/4" outside both edges. Stencil on a chain of squares using template #1. Begin at the corners and move the template in. You may have to adjust the size of the squares slightly to make them come out even. Draw in the Pumpkin Seeds freehand. Use a ruler to mark the Chevrons.

5. The outside border is marked by extending the background crosshatching of the center section. See Chart A.

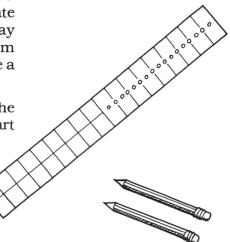

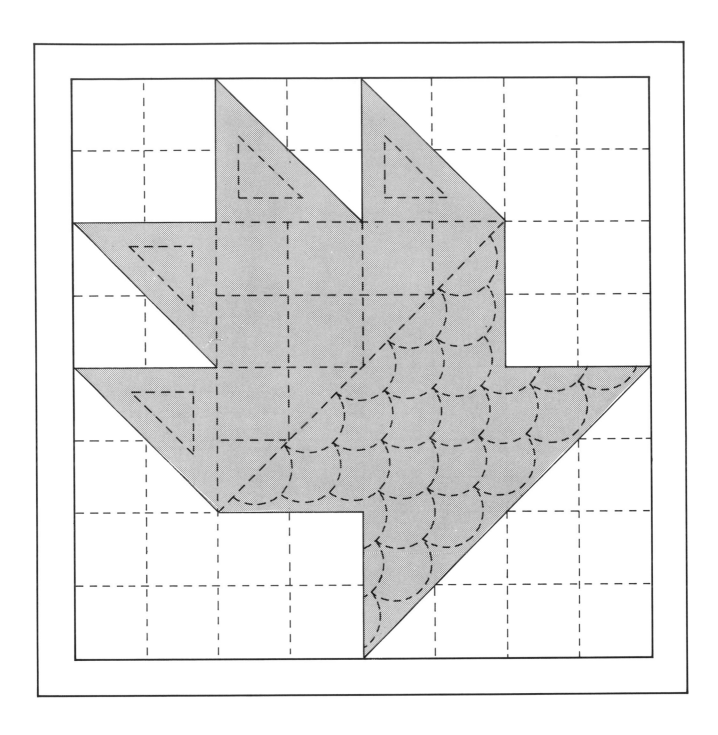

Chart C: Quilting pattern for Baskets squares. To make stencil for unpieced blocks, follow instructions on page 20. The outside solid line on the above drawing represents the edge of the stencil and is not a sewing line. Cut out the shaded area. Trace the main shape of the design on the fabric using the stencil, add other lines freehand or with a ruler.

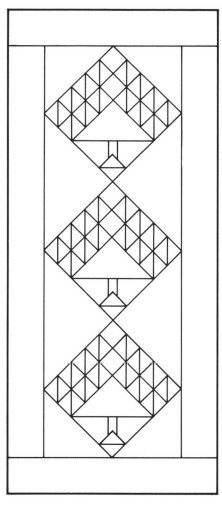

Wall Quilt

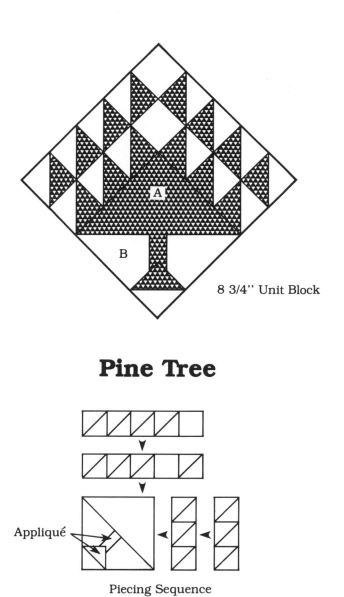

8 3/4" Unit Block

Pine Tree

Appliqué

Piecing Sequence

Color:

The Pine Tree is basically a two-color design. Green and white, or red and white unit blocks with a red or green border would make a delightful wall quilt for the Christmas season. Amish-style solids would also work well in this design.

Dimensions: 18 1/4" x 42 3/4"

Measurements for borders and pattern pieces include 1/4" seam allowances.

Materials: 45"-wide yardage

Fabric A, trees: 1/2 yd. for pattern pieces #1, #3, and #4.

Fabric B, background: 3/4 yd. for pattern pieces #1, #2, #3, #5 and #6.

Fabric C, borders and backing: 1 3/8 yd.

Directions:

1. Cut out and piece three Pine Tree unit blocks.

2. Cut four each of set pieces #5 and #6 from fabric B.

3. Set the unit blocks and set pieces together as pictured. (See "Sets" on page 13.)

4. Read the section on "Finishing" on page 16, then choose the best method for finishing your piece. The example pictured on page 40 was quilted, bound, and hung with a rod pocket and dowel.

5. Cut border strips and sew them to the pieced section with straight-sewn corners.

For a wall quilt mounted on wooden stretcher bar frame:

Cut two 5" x 37 1/4" strips.
Cut two 5" x 23 1/4" strips.

For a wall quilt to be quilted, bound, and hung with a rod
    pocket and dowel:

Cut two 3 1/2" x 18 3/4" strips.
Cut two 3 1/2" x 37 1/4" strips.

6. Finish using one of the methods outlined on page 16.

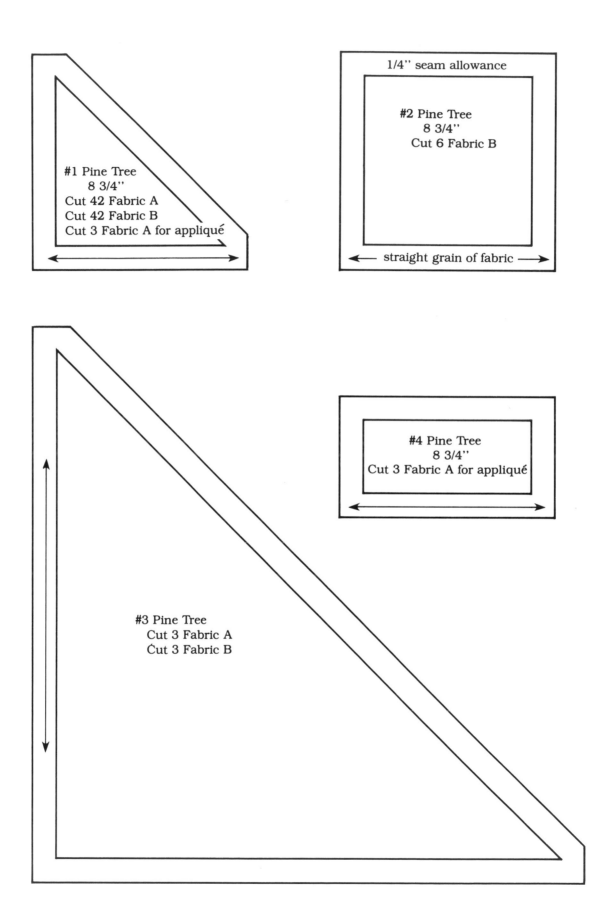

#1 Pine Tree
8 3/4"
Cut 42 Fabric A
Cut 42 Fabric B
Cut 3 Fabric A for appliqué

1/4" seam allowance

#2 Pine Tree
8 3/4"
Cut 6 Fabric B

straight grain of fabric

#4 Pine Tree
8 3/4"
Cut 3 Fabric A for appliqué

#3 Pine Tree
Cut 3 Fabric A
Cut 3 Fabric B

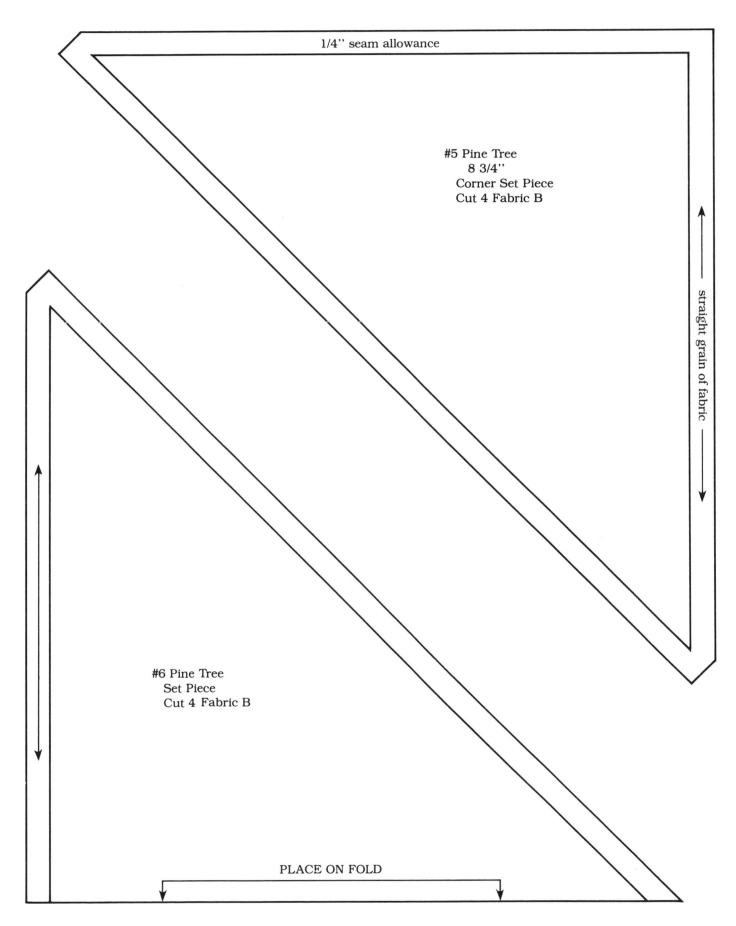

1/4" seam allowance

#5 Pine Tree
8 3/4"
Corner Set Piece
Cut 4 Fabric B

straight grain of fabric

#6 Pine Tree
Set Piece
Cut 4 Fabric B

PLACE ON FOLD

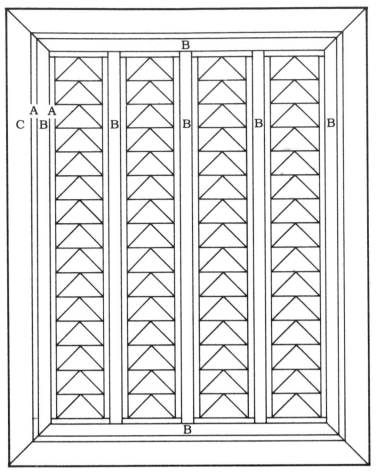

Unit

Flying Geese I

Piecing Diagram

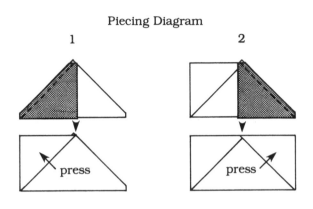

Wall Quilt

Color:

The Flying Geese I design changes when different fabric and color combinations are used. The example on page 38 has bright solid colored "geese" against a muslin background. The background could just as well be dark, or prints could be used instead of solids.

Dimensions: 45" x 54"

Measurements for borders and pattern pieces include 1/4" seam allowances.

Materials:

Fabric A: 3/4 yd. for A borders
Fabric B; 1 5/8 yd. background fabric for B and C borders and pattern piece #2.
Fabric C: 1 yd. total for "geese" (pattern piece #1)
1 5/8 yds. for backing
Batting, binding and thread to finish.

Directions:

1. Cut and piece 60 "geese" units.
2. Join "geese" in four strips of 15 units each.
3. Cut border strips and lattice pieces.

Fabric A: "A" Lattice pieces
Cut eight 1 1/4" x 42 1/2" strips.
Cut eight 1 1/4" x 7 3/5" strips.

"A" Borders
Cut two 1 1/4" x 45 1/2" strips.
Cut two 1 1/4" x 54 1/2" strips.

Fabric B: "B" Lattice strips
Cut three 2" x 44" strips.

"B" Borders
Cut two 2" x 45 1/2" strips.
Cut two 2" x 54 1/2" strips.

"C" Borders
Cut two 3 3/4" x 45 1/2" strips.
Cut two 3 3/4" x 54 1/2" strips.

4. Add "A" lattices to each pieced "geese" section as pictured.
5. Join these four units together with "B" lattices to complete pieced section of quilt.
6. Sew "B", "A" and "C" border strips together to form four striped border units.
7. Sew border units to pieced section of quilt and miter the corners. (See "Mitering" on page 15.)
8. Finish in one of the ways discussed on page 16.

Flying Geese I Pattern Sheet

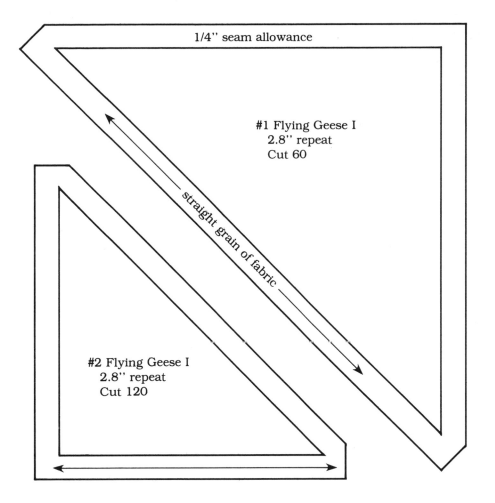

1/4" seam allowance

#1 Flying Geese I
2.8" repeat
Cut 60

straight grain of fabric

#2 Flying Geese I
2.8" repeat
Cut 120

Flying Geese II Pattern Sheet

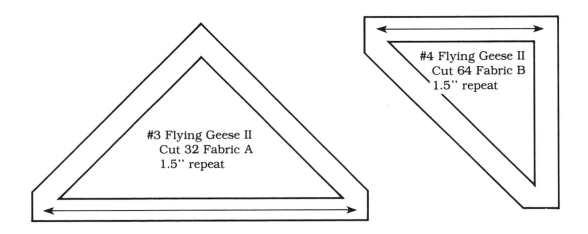

#4 Flying Geese II
Cut 64 Fabric B
1.5" repeat

#3 Flying Geese II
Cut 32 Fabric A
1.5" repeat

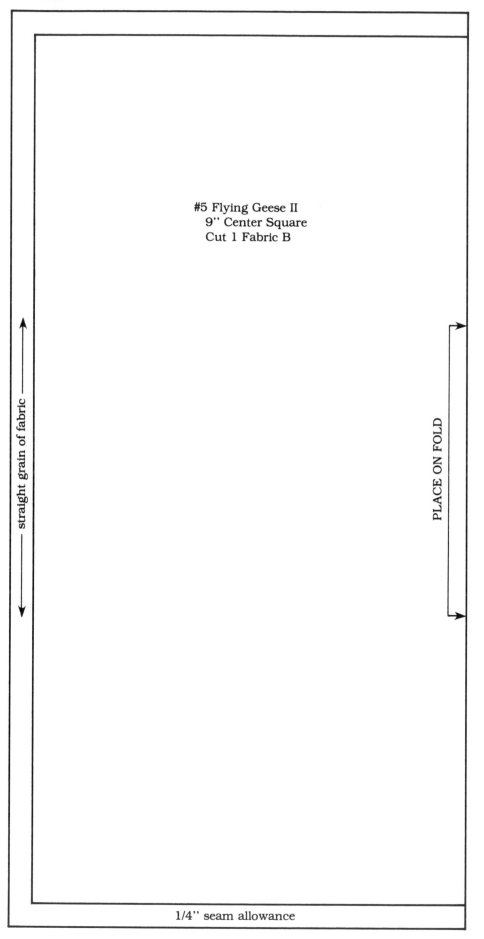

#5 Flying Geese II
9" Center Square
Cut 1 Fabric B

straight grain of fabric

PLACE ON FOLD

1/4" seam allowance

Wall Quilt

1.5"

Unit

Flying Geese II

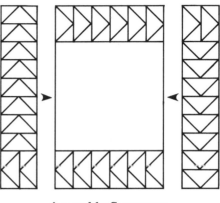

Assembly Sequence

Color:

The unpieced center square of this wall quilt is a perfect place to feature intricate quilting. Design your own motif or use Nancy Dice's Feather Wreath design on page 53. Two fabrics were used for the Flying Geese II design pictured on page 40. Vary the design by using scraps for the "geese", or make the triangles of brightly colored plain fabrics against a dark background.

Dimensions: 20" x 20"

Measurements for borders and pattern pieces include 1/4" seam allowances.

Materials: 45"-wide yardage

Fabric A: 1/4 yd. dark print or solid for "geese" (pattern piece #3)

Fabric B: 7/8 yd. background fabric for pieces #4 and #5, and borders

7/8 yd. unbleached muslin for lining

5/8 yd. thin batting (need 22" square)

4 - 20" wooden stretcher bars
    or

1 - 20" dowel or flat stick and binding to finish as a quilted hanging

Directions:

1. Cut and sew 32 "geese" units. See piecing diagram on page 64.

2. Cut a 9" center square from the background fabric using pattern piece #5.

3. Sew the "geese" together in border units, then sew those units to the center square as shown in the assembly sequence.

4. Read the section on "Finishing" on page 16. Choose the best method for finishing your wall quilt. The example shown on page 40 was quilted and then mounted on a wooden stretcher bar frame.

5. Cut the border strips and sew them to the pieced section with straight sewn corners. (See "Borders" on page 14.)

For a wall quilt mounted on a stretcher bar frame:

Cut two 5 1/2" x 15 1/2" strips.

Cut two 5 1/2" x 26 1/2" strips.

For a wall quilt to be quilted, bound and hung with a dowel and rod pocket:

Cut two 3 1/2" x 15 1/2" strips.

Cut two 3 1/2' x 21 1/2" strips.

6. Mark and quilt the Feather Wreath design found on page 53 in the center square. Add diagonal filler quilting in the borders, and quilt 1/4" inside of the seams on each of the "geese" triangles, and the center square. Read the sections on quilting, stencils and marking that begins on page 19 for help with this process.

7. Finish wall quilt using one of the methods outlined on page 16.

Pillow Possibilities

Most of the wall quilt patterns in this book can be adapted to make patchwork decorator pillows. Placed on chairs, beds and sofas, patchwork pillows can carry color and design themes, established with a wall quilt, throughout a room.

Included here are design suggestions for seven pillows made from templates provided for the wall quilts. Each suggestion is accompanied by a line drawing of a possible pillow top. Color photos of the finished pillows are found on pages 38, 39 and on the back cover. If you plan to make pillows to match a wall quilt, cut the pieces for the pillow patchwork at the same time you cut those for the larger project. You will find the fabric amounts given for each wall quilt usually allow for one or two pillow tops. For finishing the pillow, refer to the materials list provided here. It is the same for both fourteen- and sixteen-inch pillows.

Following the "Materials" and the "Design Suggestions" list is the section on "Pillow Construction." After borders are added to the patchwork, finishing is the same for all the pillows. The method outlined is for a knife-edged pillow with a piped edge and hand-sewn closing. I don't use zippers or other closures because I like the uncluttered look of a plain pillow back. I learned how to put piping on a pillow from Glendora Hutson, a well-known designer and quilting teacher in Berkeley, California. Her technique is surprisingly simple and gives such a finished, professional look that it is well worth the effort. For other pillow treatments (ruffles, boxing, zippers, etc.), I have found the Sunset book *How to Make Pillows* very helpful.

Materials

To finish a 14" or 16" knife-edged pillow with piping, you will need:
Patchwork design block
1/2 yd. fabric for pillow back and front borders
1/2 yd. unbleached muslin for lining
2 yds. covered upholstery piping
Thread to match piping
14" or 16" pillow form
Zipper foot for your sewing machine

Pillow Design Suggestions

1. Make a 14" Log Cabin pillow using the templates found on page 28. Piece four 5" Log Cabin blocks, two Block I's and two Block II's. Piecing directions begin on page 26. Sew the four blocks together to form a 10" square for the pillow top. Four different designs can be made from these blocks just by changing the arrangements of light and dark (see illustration p. 68). Add borders.

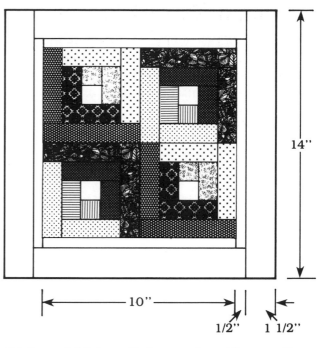

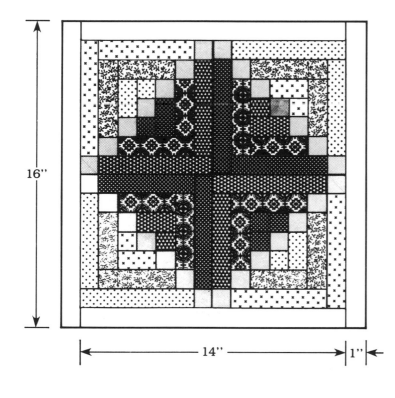

2. Make a 16" Log Cabin with a Chain pillow using the templates on page 33. Piece four blocks, two Block I's and two Block II's. Piecing instructions are on page 33. Set the four blocks together to form a 14" square. Try the four different arrangements of light and dark for this pillow, too, before you sew the blocks together and add borders.

3. Make a 16" Pineapple pillow using the templates on pages 35 and 36 and the piecing instructions on page 34. Make one 12" block for the pillow top. Add borders.

Note: Remember to add 1/4" seam allowances to all finished border dimensions.

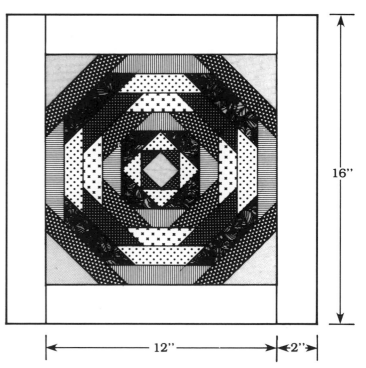

4. Piece the top for a 14" Sunshine and Shadow pillow using the template and piecing instructions on pages 43 and 44. Make one Unit C for the pillow top. Add borders.

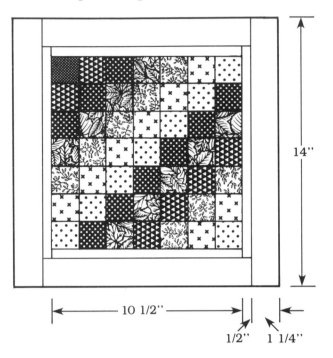

5. To make a 14" Baskets pillow, use the templates on pages 56 and 57. Piece one unit block; add four triangles to set it "on point" (use set piece #7). Add borders. Use the quilting designs given on pages 59 and 60 for the Baskets quilt or leave the pillow top unquilted.

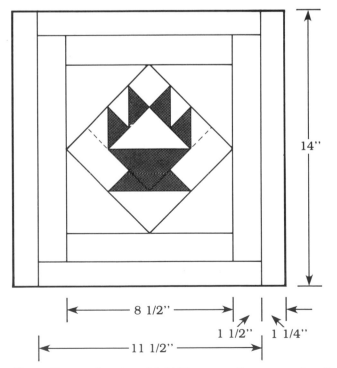

Note: Remember to add 1/4" seam allowances to all finished border dimensions.

6. To make a 16" Pine Tree pillow, use the templates on pages 62 and 63 to piece one unit block. Add four triangles (set piece #5) to set the block on point. Add borders.

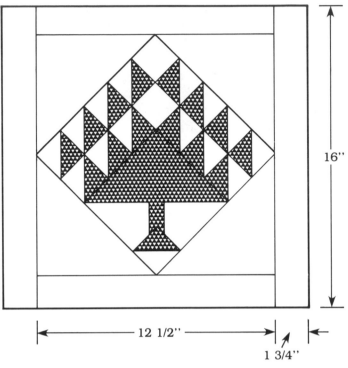

7. To make a 16" Flying Geese II pillow, piece 24 "geese" units using templates #3 and #4 on page 65. Cut a 6" square (use set piece #5 from the Baskets pattern on page 66) for the center. Set the "geese" and square together in a way similar to the piecing diagram for the Flying Geese II wall quilt on page 67. Add borders.

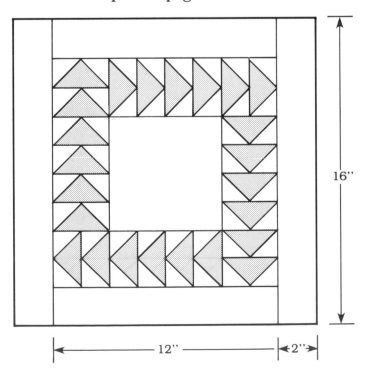

Pillow Construction

1. Make a patchwork design for the pillow front. Press.

2. Add appropriate borders. Borders function as a frame to the pieced design, keep the shapes from distorting over the curved edges of the pillow, and provide unpieced edges on which to sew the piping. Choose a border treatment for your pillow. Do you want single or multiple borders? Plain fabrics or prints? How about stripes? Corners can be mitered or straight sewn. See "Borders" on page 14. Consider piping in a contrasting color to be a visual border as well.

To figure border widths, subtract the finished dimension of the patchwork from the finished size of the pillow.

Example: 16" (finished pillow size) - 12" (finished patchwork) = 4" left for borders

4" ÷ 2 sides = 2" wide borders on each side

Remember to add 1/4" seam allowances to all finished border dimensions. Cut border strips on the straight grain of the fabric.

3. Cut pillow backing. Back and borders can be of the same or different fabrics. For texture and good durability, consider using brushed denim, corduroy, or other pants-weight fabric for the pillow back. Cut the pillow back 3/4" to 1" larger all the way around than the pillow front.

4. From unbleached muslin, cut a lining for both the pillow front and back. The lining for the front should extend about an inch beyond the edge of the borders. The lining for the back is cut the same size as the pillow back. Press and pin baste the linings to the wrong sides of the front and the back. If you wish to quilt the pillow front or back, place a thin batt between the outside layer and the lining and follow the quilting instructions that begin on page 19.

5. Fabric-covered upholstery piping is available in many colors. It can usually be found in stores that carry upholstery and drapery fabric. Lightweight, packaged piping is fine for pincushions and clothing. The thicker upholstery weight makes a better edge for pillows. Follow the five steps ("A" through "E") to make a piped edge for your pillow. Read the directions before you begin and refer to the illustrations for further help.

A. Sew the right side of the piping to the right side of the pillow front. The wrong side of the piping is sewn with a commercial chain stitch. The right side of the piping exposes a regular straight stitch. Work with the chain-stitched side up. Use a zipper foot, a regular stitch length (8 to 10 per inch), and a 1/4" seam allowance. Place one end of the piping in the middle of one side of the pillow front, matching raw edges. Begin stitching one inch from the end of the piping. Backtack. Sew right on top of the chain stitches. At the corners, clip the seam allowance on the piping to help make a graceful freehand curve as illustrated. Continue stitching around the corner. Stop stitching (with the needle down) about two inches before the point where the two ends of the piping will meet. The ends should overlap an inch. Trim away excess length. Open the stitches on the top piping end for 1 1/2". Trim the exposed cord so the two cord ends butt up to one another. Fold under the raw edge of the top piping cover, and tuck it neatly around the bit of piping that was left unstitched.(See Figure 49.) Continue the line of machine stitching to close.

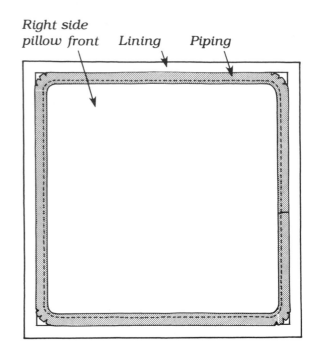

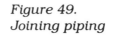

Step A: Sew the piping to the pillow front

Figure 49.
Joining piping

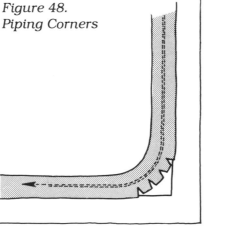

Figure 48.
Piping Corners

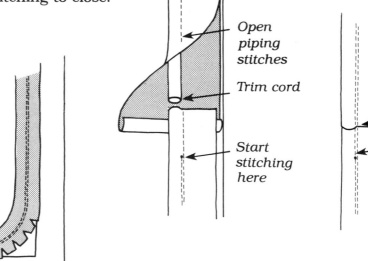

Step B: On back of pillow front, stitch close to piping on the one side that is to remain open for stuffing.

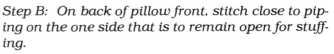

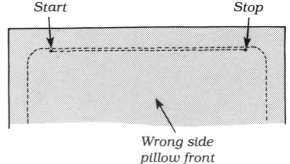

B. Choose one side of the pillow to leave open for stuffing. On the side that is to remain open and on the wrong side of the pillow front, stitch as close to the piping as possible.

C. With right sides together, pin baste the pillow front to the pillow back. Using the existing stitching line as a guide, sew the front and back together. Work with the wrong side of the pillow front toward you—the back side has no stitching lines to follow. Remember to leave an opening for stuffing.

D. Turn the pillow over. On the wrong side of the back, stitch as close to the piping as possible without sewing through it. Use the existing stitching as a guide. Leave an opening for stuffing. This third line of sewing may seem superfluous to you, but it is this extra step that will give the pillow a professionally finished look.

E. Now, trim the excess fabric along the edges to match the raw edge of the piping. Turn the pillow right side out. Check for unwanted stitches showing along the piping. If you can see stitches on the piping, especially at the corners, turn the pillow wrong side out again and sew closer to the piping where necessary.

Step C: Stitch pillow front to pillow back. Stitch closer to piping than previous row of stitches. Leave one side open.

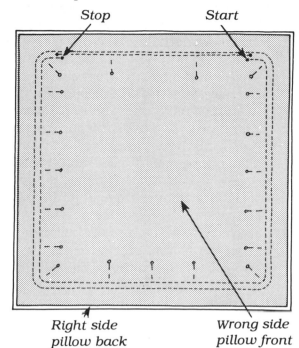

Right side
pillow back

Wrong side
pillow front

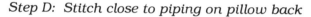

Step D: Stitch close to piping on pillow back

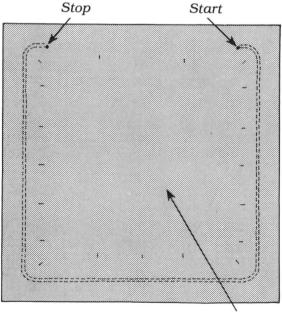

Wrong side
pillow back

6. Turn the pillow right side out. Insert the pillow form, and hand stitch the opening closed with a blind stitch. See Figure 50.

Figure 50. Hand sewn closing

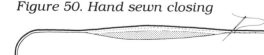

Pillow Forms

I usually buy ready-made polyester pillow forms for my pillows. A good form will measure one inch larger from side seam to side seam than the pillow for which it is intended. Thus a 16" pillow form should actually measure 17". I try to plan pillows to fit available form sizes (mostly 12", 14", 16" or 18" squares). If a pillow is an odd size (15") or a shape that is not square, the construction of a pillow form becomes necessary. It is not hard, and if you have batting scraps to use, can be a lot cheaper than buying manufactured forms.

To make a pillow form, you will need thick, bonded polyester batting (this can be found in quilt or fabric stores on large rolls and can be purchased by the yard), a bag of loose polyester stuffing or batting scraps, needle and thread.

Directions:

1. Cut two pieces of bonded batting to measure one inch larger than the finished pillow. Whip stitch the edges together leaving an eight to ten inch opening on one side for stuffing. Figure 51.
2. Insert the unfinished pillow form in the pillow casing, matching corners and opening left for stuffing.
3. Evenly stuff loose polyester between the two layers of thick batting. The smooth surface of the bonded batting will help keep the pillow from feeling lumpy. Fill it as full as you like, then whip stitch the bonded batting closed. Close the pillow as described above.

Figure 51. Making your own pillow form.

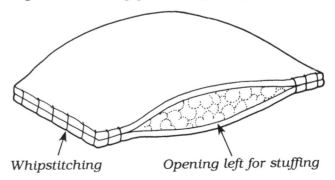

Whipstitching   *Opening left for stuffing*

Bibliography

Books:

Beyer, Jinny, Patchwork Patterns, *Virginia: EPM Publications, Inc., 1979.*

Bishop, Robert and Elizabeth Safanda, A Gallery of Amish Quilts, *New York: E.P. Dutton & Co., Inc., 1976.*

Gutcheon, Beth, The Perfect Patchwork Primer, *Baltimore: Penguin Books, Inc., 1974.*

Haders, Phyllis, Sunshine and Shadow, The Amish and Their Quilts, *New York: Universe Books, 1976.*

Hall, Carrie A. and Rose G. Krestinger, The Romance of the Patchwork Quilt, *(Caldwell, Idaho: Caxton Printers, Ltd., 1935. (Reprinted by Dover Publications, New York, 1988: ISBN 0-486-25792-4.)*

Holstein, Jonathan, The Pieced Quilt, An American Design Tradition, *Greenwich, Connecticut: New York Graphic Society Ltd., 1973.*

Johannah, Barbara, The Quick Quiltmaking Handbook, *Menlo Park, California: Pride of the Forest Press, 1979.*

Leman, Bonnie and Judy Martin, Log Cabin Quilts, *Denver, Colorado: Moon Over the Mountain Publishing Co., 1980.*

Leman, Bonnie and Judy Martin, Taking the Math Out of Making Patchwork Quilts, *Denver, Colorado: Moon Over the Mountain Publishing Co., 1981.*

McCloskey, Marsha R., Small Quilts, *Bothell, Washington: That Patchwork Place, 1982.*

Orlofsky, Patsy and Myron, Quilts in America, *New York: McGraw Hill Book Co., 1974.*

Safford, Carleton L. and Robert Bishop, America's Quilts and Coverlets, *New York: Weathervane Books, 1974*

Sunset, How to Make Pillows, *Menlo Park, California: Lane Publishing Co., 1980.*

Woodard, Thos. K. and Blanche Greenstein, Crib Quilts and Other Small Wonders, *New York: E.P. Dutton, 1981.*

Young, Blanche and Helen Young, Trip Around the World Quilts, *Oak View, California: Young Publications, 1980.*

Periodicals:

Lady's Circle Patchwork, *Lopez Publications Inc., New York.*

Quilter's Newsletter Magazine, *Leman Publications, Inc., Wheatridge, Colorado.*

Biographical Information

Marsha McCloskey has been quilting since 1970.

A graphic arts major in college, Marsha turned from printmaking to quiltmaking as motherhood and family responsibilities made the messier media impractical. The weekly "Saturday Market" in Eugene, Oregon, provided a handy outlet for her earliest quilting efforts. She found that the more quilts and small items she sold, the more she had to make to replace them. Such daily practice increased her skills as a seamstress and fabric artist. This also marked the beginning of many years of producing patchwork gift items for craft fairs and gift shops in the Northwest and California.

Marsha started teaching quiltmaking in 1975 and has taught classes and workshops in California, Oregon, Washington and British Columbia. Living now in Seattle, she teaches for quilting stores and interest groups, and is writing a series of quilt pattern books.

SMALL QUILTS, Marsha's first pattern book was published in 1982 by That Patchwork Place. WALL QUILTS is the second book in this series with several more books planned.

Metric Conversion Chart

CONVERTING INCHES TO CENTIMETERS AND YARDS TO METERS

mm — millimeters   cm — centimeters   m — meters

INCHES INTO MILLIMETERS AND CENTIMETERS
(Slightly rounded off for convenience)

inches	mm		cm	inches	cm	inches	cm	inches	cm
⅛	3mm			5	12.5	21	53.5	38	96.5
¼	6mm			5½	14	22	56	39	99
⅜	10mm	or	1cm	6	15	23	58.5	40	101.5
½	13mm	or	1.3cm	7	18	24	61	41	104
⅝	15mm	or	1.5cm	8	20.5	25	63.5	42	106.5
¾	20mm	or	2cm	9	23	26	66	43	109
⅞	22mm	or	2.2cm	10	25.5	27	68.5	44	112
1	25mm	or	2.5cm	11	28	28	71	45	114.5
1¼	32mm	or	3.2cm	12	30.5	29	73.5	46	117
1½	38mm	or	3.8cm	13	33	30	76	47	119.5
1¾	45mm	or	4.5cm	14	35.5	31	79	48	122
2	50mm	or	5cm	15	38	32	81.5	49	124.5
2½	65mm	or	6.5cm	16	40.5	33	84	50	127
3	75mm	or	7.5cm	17	43	34	86.5		
3½	90mm	or	9cm	18	46	35	89		
4	100mm	or	10cm	19	48.5	36	91.5		
4½	115mm	or	11.5cm	20	51	37	94		

YARDS TO METERS
(Slightly rounded off for convenience)

yards	meters	yards	meters	yards	meters	yards	meters	yards	meters
⅛	0.15	2⅛	1.95	4⅛	3.80	6⅛	5.60	8⅛	7.45
¼	0.25	2¼	2.10	4¼	3.90	6¼	5.75	8¼	7.55
⅜	0.35	2⅜	2.20	4⅜	4.00	6⅜	5.85	8⅜	7.70
½	0.50	2½	2.30	4½	4.15	6½	5.95	8½	7.80
⅝	0.60	2⅝	2.40	4⅝	4.25	6⅝	6.10	8⅝	7.90
¾	0.70	2¾	2.55	4¾	4.35	6¾	6.20	8¾	8.00
⅞	0.80	2⅞	2.65	4⅞	4.50	6⅞	6.30	8⅞	8.15
1	0.95	3	2.75	5	4.60	7	6.40	9	8.25
1⅛	1.05	3⅛	2.90	5⅛	4.70	7⅛	6.55	9⅛	8.35
1¼	1.15	3¼	3.00	5¼	4.80	7¼	6.65	9¼	8.50
1⅜	1.30	3⅜	3.10	5⅜	4.95	7⅜	6.75	9⅜	8.60
1½	1.40	3½	3.20	5½	5.05	7½	6.90	9½	8.70
1⅝	1.50	3⅝	3.35	5⅝	5.15	7⅝	7.00	9⅝	8.80
1¾	1.60	3¾	3.45	5¾	5.30	7¾	7.10	9¾	8.95
1⅞	1.75	3⅞	3.55	5⅞	5.40	7⅞	7.20	9⅞	9.05
2	1.85	4	3.70	6	5.50	8	7.35	10	9.15

AVAILABLE FABRIC WIDTHS

25"	65cm	50"	127cm
27"	70cm	54"/56"	140cm
35"/36"	90cm	58"/60"	150cm
39"	100cm	68"/70"	175cm
44"/45"	115cm	72"	180cm
48"	122cm		